"Lori Hatcher has a gift of reminding us of God's promises and character through her captivating stories and life experiences. As someone who leads an organization that offers Christian hope to hurting and confused people, I value *Refresh Your Hope* as a daily boost of encouragement to persevere in both life and ministry."

—Mark Baumgartner, founder and executive director of
    A Moment of Hope

"You're longing for renewed hope. This book will lead you to the water of hope that never fades. Biblical, practical, and authentic. Renewed hope beckons like cool water on every page."

—Lori Stanley Roeleveld, author of *Colorful Connections: 12 Questions about Race That Open Healthy Conversations*

"As a woman who has served in a lifetime of pastoral ministry alongside my husband, I am continually searching for biblically rooted, theologically sound resources to recommend to those who are wrestling with faith in the midst of deep difficulties. If the content is engaging and compelling, it's a bonus! Lori Hatcher's new devotional *Refresh Your Hope* is just what I've been searching for. Like Jesus, Lori uses the power of story to draw modern-day applications from the timeless truths of Scripture, and she does so in a winsome, relatable way. By focusing on the nature, work, and Word of God, *Refresh Your Hope* leads readers out of despair into a place of joyful faith."

—Maggie Wallem Rowe, author of *This Life We Share:
    52 Reflections on Journeying Well with God and Others*

"'Hope,' concludes Lori Hatcher, 'is the ability to look forward to the future with certainty and joyful anticipation.' In *Refresh Your Hope*, Lori gives us reason after reason to look beyond the chaos of our current times and put our trust in God, the One who is Lord of all our yesterdays, todays, and tomorrows. Like a master artist, she paints the details of hope into her book as she invites us to explore who God is, what He does, and what He says that give every evidence for us to move forward in hope."

—**Karen Wingate, author of the ECPA Award winner,** *With Fresh Eyes: 60 Insights into the Miraculously Ordinary from a Woman Born Blind*

refresh your hope

60 DEVOTIONS FOR TRUSTING GOD WITH ALL YOUR HEART

LORI HATCHER

Our Daily Bread
Publishing.

Requests for permission to quote from this book should be directed to: Permissions Department, Our Daily Bread Publishing, PO Box 3566, Grand Rapids, MI 49501, or contact us by email at permissionsdept@odb.org.

Scripture quotations, unless otherwise indicated, are taken from the Holy Bible, New International Version®, NIV®. Copyright © 1973, 1978, 1984, 2011 by Biblica, Inc.™ Used by permission of Zondervan. All rights reserved worldwide. www.zondervan.com.

Scripture quotations marked ESV are from the ESV® Bible (The Holy Bible, English Standard Version®), copyright © 2001 by Crossway, a publishing ministry of Good News Publishers. Used by permission. All rights reserved.

Scripture quotations marked NKJV are taken from the New King James Version®. Copyright © 1982 by Thomas Nelson. Used by permission. All rights reserved.

Italics in Scripture reflect the author's added emphasis.

To protect the privacy of individuals, some names, characteristics, and identifying details have been changed; others have been used with permission.

Interior design by Faceout Studio, Paul Nielsen

ISBN: 978-1-64070-212-7

Library of Congress Cataloging-in-Publication Data

Names: Hatcher, Lori, author.
Title: Refresh your hope : 60 devotions for trusting God with all your heart / Lori Hatcher.
Description: Grand Rapids, MI : Our Daily Bread Publishing, 2023. | Summary: "Sixty biblical reasons assure us that God's version of hope will order the events of our lives to refine us and make us more like His Son"-- Provided by publisher.
Identifiers: LCCN 2022025814 | ISBN 9781640702127
Subjects: LCSH: Bible--Meditations. | Hope--Religious aspects--Christianity--Prayers and devotions. | God (Christianity)--Biblical teaching.
Classification: LCC BS491.5 .H3774 2023 | DDC 242/.5--dc23/eng/20221130
LC record available at https://lccn.loc.gov/2022025814

Printed in the United States of America
23 24 25 26 27 28 29 30 / 9 8 7 6 5 4 3 2

To my precious Lord and Savior,
the only true and unwavering
source of hope

Contents

Introduction: Our Unshakable Hope Is Rooted in God 11

Part 1 | God's Nature (Who God Is)

1. God Is Good Lamentations 3:24-26 16
2. God Is Patient 1 Timothy 1:16 20
3. God Is Ever Present Isaiah 43:5 25
4. God Is Faithful Hebrews 10:23 29
5. God of Peace Philippians 4:7 33
6. God Existed before Time Psalm 90:1-2 37
7. Jesus Is Our Advocate 1 John 2:1 40
8. God Isn't Limited by Time and Space
   Deuteronomy 31:8 44
9. God Is Our Deliverer Zechariah 9:11-12 49
10. God Never Forgets Isaiah 49:15 53
11. God Knows Everything Romans 11:33 57
12. God of Never-Ending Love Titus 3:4-5 62
13. God of All Comfort Isaiah 53:3 65
14. God of Wisdom James 1:5 69
15. God Is Trustworthy Psalm 18:30 73
16. God Is Generous Psalm 84:11 77
17. God Alone Reigns Supreme 2 Chronicles 20:6 81

18. God of Covenant Love Deuteronomy 7:9 86

19. God Is on His Throne Psalm 123:1 90

20. God of Future Hope Proverbs 24:14 93

Part 2 | God's Work (What God Does)

21. God Always Hears Our Prayers Psalm 34:15 98

22. While We Were Still Sinners . . . Romans 5:8 102

23. God Will Complete His Work Philippians 1:6 106

24. The Gift of His Spirit 1 Corinthians 2:12 110

25. In the Waiting Times Galatians 4:4-5 115

26. God Commands Dry Bones to Live Ezekiel 37:3 119

27. God Graciously Waits Isaiah 30:18 123

28. He Remembers Our Sin No More Isaiah 43:25 126

29. He Renews Us Day by Day 2 Corinthians 4:16 130

30. God Welcomes Prodigals Psalm 40:2-3 134

31. He Never Lets Us Go Ephesians 1:13-14 138

32. God Never Wastes Pain Romans 5:3-5 143

33. God Restores Genesis 50:20 148

34. He Empowers Us to Share His Comfort
    2 Corinthians 1:3-4 153

35. God Enables Us to Forgive Matthew 18:21-22 157

36. He Gives More Grace James 4:6 161

37. He Sees and Remembers Our Work Hebrews 6:10 165

38. He Will Reward Our Sacrifices Matthew 19:29 160

39. He Draws Near James 4:8 173

40. God Will Sustain Us in Our Old Age Isaiah 46:4 177

Part 3 | God's Word (What God Says)

41. God's Word Always Accomplishes His Purpose
     Isaiah 55:11 182

42. Hope When You Feel Small Zechariah 4:10............. 186

43. We Are His People Psalm 100:3 190

44. We Have a Living Hope 1 Peter 1:3 193

45. We'll See Our Babies in Heaven 2 Samuel 12:23........ 197

46. God Will Never Leave Us Deuteronomy 31:8 201

47. We Will Reap a Harvest Galatians 6:9 206

48. While There Is Breath, There Is Hope
     Ecclesiastes 9:4...210

49. Every Gift Matters 1 Corinthians 12:18................... 214

50. Share the Reason for Your Hope 1 Peter 3:15............ 218

51. You Still Have Work to Do Philippians 1:23-24........ 222

52. God's Word Helps Us Battle the Enemy
     Psalm 119:147 226

53. God Offers Hope through Repentance Ezra 10:2 230

54. Our Families Don't Disqualify Us Psalm 42 234

55. Our Faith Is Reasonable 2 Peter 1:16 239

56. Standing Strong during Trials 2 Timothy 4:17 243

57. Sowing Tears, Reaping Joy Psalm 126:5-6.............. 247

58. Jesus Will Return Luke 21:27 251

59. Goodbyes Aren't Forever 1 Thessalonians 4:17 255

60. Incomparable Glory Awaits Us Romans 8:18 258

     How to Have a Relationship with Christ 263

     Notes 265

     About the Author 269

Introduction

Our Unshakable Hope
Is Rooted in God

**May the God of hope fill you with
all joy and peace as you trust in him,
so that you may overflow with hope
by the power of the Holy Spirit.**

ROMANS 15:13

The poet Emily Dickinson wrote,

> "Hope" is the thing with feathers
> That perches in the soul
> And sings the tune without the words
> And never stops—at all.

In four simple lines she captured the essence of what lifts every human being out of bed in the morning, moves us through our days, and enables us to persevere when life gets hard.

We hope we'll accomplish something meaningful. We hope someone will love us. We hope our lives will be free from pain. And if it's not, we hope tomorrow will be a better day.

For many, hope is nothing more than a wish. A yearning for something our heart desires. An expectancy that we'll gain the object of our affection. This type of wishful hope rises and falls with the winds of chance and circumstance. It has no solid basis and is usually tied to something or someone temporal.

Thousands of years before Emily Dickinson penned her famous lines, another writer described a different source of hope—a constant and sure One. "May the God of hope fill you with all joy and peace as you trust in him," the apostle Paul wrote, "so that you may overflow with hope by the power of the Holy Spirit" (Romans 15:13).

J. I. Packer, in his book *Never beyond Hope*, differentiates between worldly and biblical hope. "Optimism is a wish without warrant; Christian hope is a certainty, guaranteed by God himself. Optimism reflects ignorance as to whether good things will ever actually come. Christian hope expresses knowledge that every day of his life, and every moment beyond it, the believer can say with truth, on the basis of God's own commitment, that the best is yet to come."[1]

The concept of hope, then, is a biblical one. The word appears 158 times in the New International Version of the Bible. These verses describe three sources of sure and certain hope: God's character, God's work, and God's Word.

"No one who hopes in you will ever be put to shame" (Psalm 25:3).

"For what you have done I will always praise you in the presence of your faithful people. And I will hope in your name, for your name is good" (Psalm 52:9).

"You are my refuge and my shield; I have put my hope in your word" (Psalm 119:114).

Every day we have a choice where to look for hope—to created things or to our Creator. The world tells us to hope in money, luck, determination, relationships, skills, and our own abilities. God tells us to look to Him.

The world disappoints us—again and again—but God will never fail us. The hope He offers doesn't rise and fall with changing circumstances. It is solid and secure.

God's version of hope doesn't promise to deliver our personal definition of happiness. It assures us that He'll order the events of our lives to refine us and make us more like His Son. Only there will we find the deep and abiding joy we crave.

Charles Haddon Spurgeon once shared that New Zealanders have a word for hope that signifies "the swimming thought." He used the term to describe the hope God offers, "because when all other thoughts are drowned, hope still swims."[2]

I pray that the sixty biblical reasons I share in this book, and thousands more tucked into the pages of Scripture, will "fill you with all joy and peace" and cause you to "overflow with hope by the power of the Holy Spirit" (Romans 15:13).

May hope swim in your life forever.

Part 1

God's Nature
(Who God Is)

1

God Is Good

**I say to myself, "The LORD is my portion;
therefore I will wait for him." The LORD
is good to those whose hope is in him,
to the one who seeks him; it is good to wait
quietly for the salvation of the LORD.**

LAMENTATIONS 3:24–26

Romeo, my friend Alicia's Rhodesian ridgeback, was amazingly well-trained. His great size and fearsome appearance demanded it. Known as lion hunters on their native continent of Africa, Rhodesian ridgebacks were recognized for their ability to harass a lion while staying out of its reach until a hunter could shoot it.

Romeo's ancestors may have been lion hunters, but he was a gentle giant. Although he weighed more than one hundred pounds and was tall enough to rest his front paws on his owner's shoulders, he was docile and, at times, cowardly. Loud noises sent him scurrying behind Alicia's chair as she sat in her home office.

Nevertheless, because he had the size and strength to injure someone, Alicia knew she had to train him well. She taught him to walk on a leash without pulling and sit and stay on command. To avoid a tussle over food, she taught him she was master over his daily portion. He was not permitted to dive in until she said, "Okay."

To train Romeo to wait for his food, she commanded him to sit and stay. Then, with one hand on his chest, she set his bowl in front of him. "Wait," she said. Whenever he moved, she restrained him. "Wait . . ."

At first, she waited thirty seconds or so to release him. Then she said, "Okay, Romeo. Good boy!" She lifted her hand from his chest and allowed him to eat.

As he gained self-control and learned to trust that Alicia would allow him to eat—every time—he no longer needed her hand on his chest to restrain him. She gradually increased the time between when she set the bowl before him and when she allowed him to dig in. Eventually, she could put his food down and leave the room, knowing he'd wait quietly.

One day she commanded him to sit and stay, then set down his bowl.

"Mom," her daughter called from upstairs, "can you help me get a game down from the closet?" Alicia ran upstairs, snagged the game from the top shelf, and headed back down. On her way to the kitchen, she glanced out the window and noticed the mail carrier making his rounds. She stepped outside, retrieved the mail, and came back in. Settling into her chair, she flipped through the mail.

"Mom," her daughter called again, this time from the kitchen. "Come look at Romeo."

"Oh gosh," Alicia said, jumping up from her chair. "I forgot to release him."

She rounded the corner to see her trusting and hopeful dog sitting right where she'd left him—waiting in front of his food bowl, saliva dripping from his jowls and forming a puddle at his feet.

In this world, we often use the word *hope* as synonymous with an optimistic emotion, but in the Bible, two Old Testament words translated "hope" (*yakhal* and *qavah)* refer to waiting.

In Lamentations 3:21, "Yet this I call to mind and therefore I have hope," Jeremiah used the word *yakhal.* This is the same word translated "will wait for" in verse 24. "I say to myself, 'The LORD is my portion; therefore I will wait for him.'"

The translation of these two words reminds us that biblical hope—waiting in expectation—doesn't require feeling optimistic about whatever's going on in our lives. Our hope is firmly rooted in God's character and faithfulness to bring about a future good.

Thankfully, because God is good, He never forgets us like Alicia forgot Romeo. He doesn't wander away, get distracted by what's going on elsewhere, or direct His attention to someone or something else. He's always working within His nature to accomplish His perfect will for us (Philippians 2:13). When we place our hope in His good nature and seek Him with all our hearts, we can wait in quiet hope for Him to fulfill all His good purposes for us.

Take Heart

God's character and good nature enable us to wait in confident hope for Him to bring about good in our lives.

From the Heart

Father, I'm so grateful that you are unquestioningly good. Because your nature doesn't change, when the circumstances of my life are hard, I can rest in hope. During the waiting times, I can look back on your goodness— to me and to believers down through the ages—and smile at the future. Remind me during the trying times how you've faithfully cared for me all the days of my life. In the strong name of Jesus I ask, amen.

2

God Is Patient

**But for that very reason I was shown mercy
so that in me, the worst of sinners, Christ
Jesus might display his immense patience as
an example for those who would believe in
him and receive eternal life.**

1 TIMOTHY 1:16

When you're so bad they don't even want you in prison, you know you're bad.

Really, really bad.

That was Jimmy MacPhee.

Jimmy didn't start out bad. In high school he was a two-sport athlete who made good grades and enjoyed classes. When a part-time job gave him money and freedom, he made new friends who cared little about school. His new lifestyle included fast cars, promiscuous sex, a plethora of drugs—and an armed bank robbery. Jimmy pulled the trigger, critically wounding one man and killing another.

A judge sentenced him to die in South Carolina's electric chair. He was twenty years old.

"I had become everything I despised," Jimmy said. Angry. Violent. Condemned.

But God hadn't forsaken him.

God sent Frankie San, a soft-spoken man who served as the jail's volunteer librarian, to shine the light of Christ into Jimmy's dark cell.

"I love you, and Jesus loves you," Frankie said through the bars. "He doesn't care what crimes you've committed. He will forgive you if you let Him."

Jimmy wasn't interested.

While he awaited execution, a technicality in the law commuted his sentence from death to life in prison, but even this lifesaving grace didn't soften Jimmy's heart. Each year he grew more angry and violent.

Although Frankie San continued to speak words of life and hope whenever he delivered books to Jimmy's cell, he sank deeper into a mindset of rage and hopelessness. A final vicious attack on a guard removed him from the prison population and sentenced him to solitary confinement for the duration of his sentence. Jimmy was forty years old.

There in his ten-by-ten cell, he took stock of his life. He'd spent two decades in prison and had nothing to show for it except death and destruction. Hopeless, he wrote to Frankie San, his old friend from death row. "I'm tired of my life. I desperately want something different, but I don't know what."

Frankie wrote back and reiterated the message he'd spoken to Jimmy twenty years before: "I love you, and Jesus Christ loves you.

He doesn't care what crimes you committed. He will forgive you if you let Him. Give all your pain, anger, and brokenness to God, and he will heal you."

This time, Jimmy took Frankie's words to heart. "I bowed my head, and as the tears flowed, I asked God to take what little life I hadn't destroyed and do with it what He would. I prayed, confessed my sins, and asked His forgiveness for all the pain I'd caused."

Silently, almost imperceptibly, a peace settled over his soul. Despite his sentence to spend the rest of his life in solitary confinement, Jimmy knew he'd never be alone again. For the first time in years, he felt a flicker of hope.

Saul of Tarsus followed a very different path than Jimmy. Born a Roman citizen and taught under the esteemed Gamaliel, Saul was an up-and-coming wonder boy. His extensive knowledge of the Torah allowed him to preach in the finest synagogues. He prided himself on his educational and professional credentials.

Yet his heart was as violent as Jimmy's. In his religious zeal, he stood in solidarity while an angry mob stoned Stephen the apostle. "I was once a blasphemer and a persecutor and a violent man," he confessed in 1 Timothy 1:13. "I persecuted the followers of this Way [Christians] to their death, arresting both men and women and throwing them into prison" (Acts 22:4). As was the case for Jimmy, Paul's anger and violence almost consumed him.

"But when God, who set me apart from my mother's womb and called me by his grace, was pleased to reveal his Son in me," Paul testified in Galatians 1:15–16, he was transformed. Paul went from denying Christ to proclaiming Him.

After his conversion, Jimmy threw himself into study. He read his Bible and other books for hours each day. Little by little the truth of God's Word changed him from a blaspheming murderer to a Spirit-filled peacemaker.

Sixteen years after he was sentenced to solitary confinement and twenty-five years after he was sentenced to die in the electric chair, Jimmy was released into the prison population. He continued to apply for parole, but most agreed he'd probably spend the rest of his life behind bars.

Jimmy invested the next twenty years into becoming a writer, speaker, teacher, and mentor to troubled younger prisoners and gang members. He led many men to the Lord as a servant leader. In 2017, he was chosen as one of only a few inmates to pursue a Bible college education from Columbia International University through its prison initiative. There he was trained to be both a missionary and a peacemaker to the most dangerous prison yards in South Carolina.

Paul's transformation, described by the awestruck disciples, was equally glorious: "The man who formerly persecuted us is now preaching the faith he once tried to destroy" (Galatians 1:23). Paul testified of Christ to Caesar, wrote thirteen books of the New Testament, and planted numerous churches throughout Asia. As the self-proclaimed "worst of sinners," Paul shared his story as living proof of God's immense patience for those who think they are beyond redemption.

Paul became the apostle to the Gentiles and partnered with the disciples he once persecuted, evangelizing most of the known world. Jimmy became an ambassador to the prison population, sharing Christ with the inmates he once terrorized.

Paul was executed by Nero around AD 67 after spending the remainder of his life in prison. Jimmy was released on March 18, 2020, after forty-five years and seventeen parole board hearings.

Now an ordained minister and founder of On the Rock Ministries, Jimmy speaks in churches, youth groups, and prisons. His message brings life and hope to those who wonder if God's patience extends to them.[1]

"If He did it for me," Jimmy says, "He can do it for you."

Take Heart

If you or someone you love feel God's Spirit drawing you, no matter what you've done, it's not too late. God's patience makes room for you.

From the Heart

Father, sometimes I lose heart when I see the path my friends and loved ones are taking. I want them to surrender their lives to you, but I see no evidence that you're at work. All I see is death and destruction. Thank you for Paul's and Jimmy's testimonies that prove that you are infinitely patient and always at work, even when I can't see it. Soften my loved ones' hearts toward you. Deepen their desire for your ways. Give me hope, as I continue to pray, that, one day, your patience will bring about their salvation and transformation. In the strong name of Jesus I ask, amen.

3

God Is Ever Present

Do not be afraid, for I am with you.

ISAIAH 43:5

There's nothing like the sound of a child in the throes of a nightmare.

I heard that sound late one night. I'd tucked my grandchildren into bed, cleaned up the kitchen, and settled onto the couch for a few quiet moments when a scream erupted from the bedroom.

My daughter had warned me. Lauren, the oldest, had been experiencing nightmares. Still, I wasn't prepared for the heart-pounding rush of adrenaline that propelled me off the couch and down the hallway. I nearly collided with Lauren in the doorway to her bedroom.

Hair tousled from sleep and eyes wide with fear, she tumbled into my embrace. I couldn't understand her panicked words, but I could feel her heart pounding.

"It's okay, sweetie," I said. "Gigi's here. You don't have to be afraid."

With my arm around her shoulders, I walked her back to bed, then sat beside her. Holding her close to quiet her frantic movements,

I prayed, "Dear Jesus, calm Lauren's heart and mind. Help her not be afraid. Help her know that you are near."

She continued to cry out and point to imaginary monsters as I emptied my What-to-Do-in-Case-of-a-Nightmare bag. I sang "Jesus Loves Me." I spoke comforting words. I quoted Bible verses. I prayed again, inviting God's peace.

Finally, her cries subsided, and her heart rate slowed. I stretched out beside her, cuddled her close, and asked, "Would you like to hear a story?"

She nodded as I tucked the comforter under her chin.

By the time I finished the story of the beautiful castle in the sky, her breathing had quieted, and her eyes had closed. I hugged her gently, kissed her on the forehead, and rose to leave.

"Thank you, Gigi," she whispered. "I love you."

I can sympathize with Lauren's fright because I've experienced more than a few nightmares in my lifetime. Most of them, unfortunately, weren't caused by an overactive imagination. They were real.

I've lived through the scare of my husband's extended unemployment (twice). I've trembled while waiting for biopsy results. I've wept as Satan lured away those I love. I've wailed as death robbed our family of loved ones.

Yet in the depth of every nightmare, God has been there, wrapping me in His warm embrace and whispering truth into my frightened heart.

"It's okay," He's said, drawing me close. "I'm here. You don't have to be afraid."

Through believing friends, timely messages, and His Word, He's spoken truth into my heart. He's comforted me with His promises and banished my fears.

He's sung over me, quieting my trembling heart—leading me to understand at the deepest part of me, *Jesus loves me, this I know, for the Bible tells me so.*

He's spread the blanket of peace over my troubled soul and tucked it tightly under my chin. Holding me close in the darkest nights, He's invited me to rest in His embrace.

And He's told me stories.

"Then I saw 'a new heaven and a new earth,' for the first heaven and the first earth had passed away, and there was no longer any sea" (Revelation 21:1).

"And I heard a loud voice from the throne saying, 'Look! God's dwelling place is now among the people, and he will dwell with them. They will be his people, and God himself will be with them and be their God. "He will wipe every tear from their eyes. There will be no more death" or mourning or crying or pain, for the old order of things has passed away'" (Revelation 21:3–4).

Every time I cry out, He comforts me in my nightmare and leaves me with His peace.

My response is simple: *Thank you, Jesus. I love you.*

If you're living through a nightmare right now, know this—God is right there with you.

Because of the comfort of His presence and the assurance of an eternity with no death, mourning, crying, pain—or nightmares— you can have hope.

Take Heart

The comfort of God's presence will carry us through any nightmare we experience.

From the Heart

Father, thank you for the comforting promise of heaven, where nightmares will cease, and I'll live with you forever. Thank you also for the comfort you provide and the promise that you'll walk with me through every trial and comfort me when I cry. When I am afraid, help me trust in you. In the strong name of Jesus I pray, amen.

4

God Is Faithful

Let us hold unswervingly to the hope we profess, for he who promised is faithful.

HEBREWS 10:23

Will Peterson had grand plans of owning his own architectural firm one day. A graduate of a well-respected university, he intended to make his fortune designing innovative business structures in his hometown. He'd earn a substantial enough living to build his dream home, send his children to private college, and fund a generous retirement account.

Five years out of college, he entered a partnership with Chip, a middle-aged member of the firm he'd been working with since graduation. They borrowed money to open their own office, confident they'd earn it back within a few years. And they were well on their way—until Chip was diagnosed with leukemia.

"I don't know if I can beat this," Chip said to Will one afternoon halfway through his treatment. "But I want to ask you something. Sarah and I were never able to have kids. I'm all she's got. If something happens to me, she'll have no means of support. Promise me you'll take care of her."

"I promise," Will said.

Nine months later, Chip died.

Will kept the business afloat for a while, but soon realized he couldn't do the work of two. Because of the debt load, he couldn't afford to bring in a new partner, but he refused to declare bankruptcy.

His only choice was to close the firm. He accepted a position with the state and negotiated a debt repayment plan. Knowing Chip had emptied his savings to help start the business, he didn't have the heart to tell his grieving widow she now owed thousands of dollars. He assumed the debt himself.

Then Will sat down with Sarah and worked out a budget. The shortfall between her monthly expenses and the income she had from Chip's social security benefits added up to just under eight hundred dollars a month.

"I'll send you a check on the first of each month," he promised.

And he did—for twenty-one years.

I met Will ten years into his commitment. He hadn't built his dream home. Instead, he lived in an older house in a modest neighborhood. God had blessed him with a godly wife, two daughters, and five cats. He served his church as a deacon and taught a boy's Sunday school class.

One day, he shared the story of his commitment to Chip.

"You're crazy, man," one boy said. "I can understand wanting to help someone, but that's just too much. Why'd ya do it?"

"I made a promise to Chip—and to God," Will said. "I gave my word. I've never regretted it. I haven't had all the stuff I wanted, but God used that commitment to make me into the man I am today. He's provided everything we need. God has taken care of us."

When I think of Will, the word *faithful* comes to mind. His integrity gives me hope. Will's life stands as a shining example of the faithfulness of God reflected in His people.

Scripture shores up this reason for hope and gives it weight and history.

Joshua reminded the Israelites of God's faithfulness. He'd freed them from the Egyptians, settled them in the promised land, and granted them victory over their enemies. "Not one of all the Lord's good promises to Israel failed; every one was fulfilled," he declared in Joshua 21:45.

Solomon, centuries later, proclaimed, "Praise be to the Lord, who has given rest to his people Israel just as he promised. Not one word has failed of all the good promises he gave through his servant Moses" (1 Kings 8:56).

The writer of Hebrews agreed, calling the Jewish believers to "hold unswervingly to the hope we profess, for he who promised is faithful" (Hebrews 10:23).

Paul encouraged the Thessalonians' faith by saying, "He who calls you is faithful; he will surely do it" (1 Thessalonians 5:24 ESV).

But God's faithfulness isn't just for believers in Bible days. It has flowed through God's children down through the ages and swirls around us today. The believers who came before us form the cloud of witnesses that helped inspire modern believers like Harriet Tubman, Billy Graham, and Will. Together they testify to God's unswerving commitment to His children and model His faithfulness to a watching world.

The next time our hope wavers and our faith grows faint, we can look to those who have modeled faithfulness before us. Embracing the charge of the author of Hebrews to "throw off everything that hinders and the sin that so easily entangles," we can "run with perseverance the race marked out for us, fixing our eyes on Jesus, the pioneer and perfecter of faith" (Hebrews 12:1–2).

Because He who promised is faithful.

Take Heart

Because faithfulness is part of God's divine nature, He will not fail us. We can rest our hope in Him.

From the Heart

Father, in a world riddled with examples of unfaithfulness, your steadfast commitment to us, your children, gives me great hope. History bursts with believers' testimonies sharing example after example of how you have shown yourself faithful to them. Help me model your faithfulness to others and trust your faithfulness in my own life. When I waver, remind me that your mercies are new every morning, and your faithfulness endures forever. In the strong name of Jesus I pray, amen.

5

God of Peace

**And the peace of God, which transcends
all understanding, will guard your hearts
and your minds in Christ Jesus.**

PHILIPPIANS 4:7

The first time my husband, David, lost his job, I was undone.

When he returned home one Monday morning only an hour after he'd left for work, I knew something was seriously wrong. Was he sick? Hurt? Until he said those dreaded words aloud, *laid off* never entered my mind.

I looked at our two tiny daughters and my stomach clenched. Like the pint of blueberries I'd dropped on the kitchen floor earlier that day, my mind raced in a hundred directions.

Oh, God, how will we pay our bills? What about health insurance? Will we lose our home? Will I have to put the girls in daycare and work full time? My heart pounded, and panic flooded my chest.

Equally frantic thoughts hammered my husband. *What kind of provider are you? Your family depends on you, and you let them down. How are you going to feed those babies and take care of your wife? Who'd want to hire you anyway?*

Panic, not peace, ruled our hearts and minds.

When David returned home with the second pink slip of his life, we handled it very differently. Twenty-five years had passed, and we'd grown in our faith. We'd experienced God's loving care for more than two and a half decades, and we knew He was faithful. Our kind Father had proven himself sovereign over every detail of our lives thus far. Best of all, we'd learned to bring our needs to Him in prayer and watched Him provide.

Time and trials had taught us the principle of Philippians 4:6–7: "Do not be anxious about anything, but in every situation, by prayer and petition, with thanksgiving, present your requests to God. And the peace of God, which transcends all understanding, will guard your hearts and your minds in Christ Jesus."

This time, the first words out of my mouth weren't, "Oh, God," but "Thank you, God."

I knew the emotional climate had grown increasingly hostile at work. Although David had legitimate cause to complain, he'd feared losing his job if he did. His work was physically intense, causing him to need not one, but two surgeries to repair the rotator cuffs in his shoulders. We'd been asking God for years to move him to a new job. Apparently, this was how He planned to do it.

"Father," we prayed, "we've been asking you to provide a better job for David. Thank you for answering our prayer. Please meet our needs and direct our steps. In the strong name of Jesus we ask, amen."

I wish I could say that prayer alone was enough to steady our hearts and bolster our hope, but I can't. As the days turned into weeks, and the weeks into months, no job materialized. We had to enact the full emergency management plan of Philippians 4 to weather our unemployment storm and walk in peace.

"Finally, brothers and sisters," Paul wrote to the Philippian believers, "whatever is true, whatever is noble, whatever is right, whatever is pure, whatever is lovely, whatever is admirable—if anything is excellent or praiseworthy—think about such things" (v. 8). To enable peace to reign, we had to corral our thoughts and bring them into subjection.

We made every effort to exchange false thoughts for true ones. "It's up to us to provide," became, "God is our Provider."

We replaced condemning words (You're too old. No one wants to hire you.) with noble ones (Your experience and insight make you a strong candidate.).

When an offer from a questionable company came, David prayerfully declined it, choosing to seek to work with companies that had a reputation for doing what was right and pure.

Early one morning I read the account of Jesus feeding the five thousand. Jesus asked His disciple Philip a question that paralleled my own, "Where shall we buy bread for these people to eat?" (John 6:5). The verse that followed, "He asked this only to test him, for he already had in mind what he was going to do," reminded us that God already had a plan to meet our needs. In time He would reveal it. I copied the verse onto an index card and taped it to the napkin holder on our kitchen table. Seeing it at mealtimes helped us meditate on the promises of God.

David had several opportunities to do temporary work for kind friends. Even when the work was menial and beneath his training and education, he worked admirably and strove for excellence.

And each morning, as we walked the neighborhood and prayed, we praised God for who He was and what He was doing in our lives.

We didn't always implement the Philippian verses perfectly. Sometimes we'd sink into a pit of doubt and despair. But by praying and meditating on the true, noble, right, pure, lovely, admirable, excellent, and praiseworthy, we held panic at bay and felt the peace of God cradle our trembling hearts.

David's two periods of unemployment helped us realize that when trials enter our lives, we don't have to fall apart. We can experience the peace that defies understanding and fills our hearts with hope. As commentator Max Anders said, "Such peace is like a squad of Roman soldiers standing guard and protecting [us]."[2] With protection like this, we have nothing to fear.

Take Heart

When trials enter our lives, we don't have to panic. God has given us a hope-filled prescription for peace.

From the Heart

Father, I admit my first response to a crisis is often panic, not peace. Thank you for providing a better way through Philippians 4:6–8. Remind me to pray first, reign in my wayward thoughts, and replace them with those that are true, lovely, excellent, and praiseworthy. Help me keep my eyes on you and not my circumstances. Overshadow my heart with peace as I trust in you. In Jesus's name I pray, amen.

6

God Existed before Time

Lord, you have been our dwelling place throughout all generations. Before the mountains were born or you brought forth the whole world, from everlasting to everlasting you are God.

PSALM 90:1-2

"Americans have no concept of 'old,'" Margaret, a travel agent friend, said. "Europeans, on the other hand, they know old."

She was poking fun at me for bragging about growing up in Bristol, Rhode Island.

"My hometown hosts the oldest continuous Fourth of July Parade in history," I said. "The celebration goes all the way back to 1785. They call it the Military, Civic and Firemen's Parade. It began eighty-five years before the Fourth of July was even deemed a national holiday."[3]

And if that wasn't enough to impress her, I pulled out another fact from my Rhode Island Pride collection. "Bristol has houses that date back to 1680."

"You should see Europe," Margaret fired back. "Their buildings make your historic houses look like new construction."

When my husband, David, and I visited my daughter and son-in-law in Spain, I understood her comments. We took her advice and visited the ruins of Baelo Claudia, a Roman fishing town near the Strait of Gibraltar.

There, surrounded by jeweled blue water and Andalusia's rocky coastline, we walked on two-thousand-year-old roads. Displaying the skill and craftsmanship of the people who built the town two hundred years before Christ, a weathered basilica graced the city square. Nearby stood remnants of a municipal building, city walls and gates, three aqueducts, and a cistern.

"Margaret was right," I said. "Europeans know old."

A well-preserved statue of Trajan, the reigning emperor in 2 BC, stood in the center of the basilica. I gazed into his sightless eyes and wondered how many emperors, kings, and dictators had come and gone since his short reign. Thousands, perhaps.

My thoughts turned toward God, the King of Kings and Lord of Lords who has stood watch over the universe since before time and whose kingdom has no end. "You, LORD, reign forever," Jeremiah wrote in Lamentations 5:19, "your throne endures from generation to generation."

I suspect Jeremiah took his cue from Moses, who captured God's timelessness in Psalm 90: "Lord, you have been our dwelling place throughout all generations. Before the mountains were born or you brought forth the whole world, from everlasting to everlasting you are God" (vv. 1–2).

Did you catch that? *Before the mountains were born or you brought forth the whole world, . . . you are God.*

God, not Romans, existed before the world began. God, not government or financial institutions, has provided a dwelling place for all generations. God, not relationships, health, or wealth, has sheltered and protected His people through the ages.

While the emperor Trajan left a few historical notes and a statue, God has continued to exist in power and wonder from eternity past into eternity future—forever and ever. When the world threatens to crumble and the foundations of our culture shake, we can draw hope from Him.

God, our eternal Father, lives and reigns forever. He will not abandon us, nor will He fail. He transcends time and mortality because He created them. We can rest—unafraid and hope filled.

On the sandy shores of Spain, surrounded by ancient Roman ruins, I trumped Margaret's declaration.

"Christians know old."

Take Heart

Because God existed before time, He will be our God through and beyond time.

From the Heart

Father, I am finite, and you are infinite. Because you have no beginning and no end, I can trust you to carry me all the way through my life. Thank you for the hope and security I find in you. Though the world may end, you never will. In Jesus's name I pray, amen.

7

Jesus Is Our Advocate

**But if anybody does sin,
we have an advocate with the Father—
Jesus Christ, the Righteous One.**

1 JOHN 2:1

Sometimes my Bible reading fills me with cozy feelings of peace and well-being. Other times it takes me to strange and terrifying places. Books like Matthew, Mark, Luke, and John paint idyllic pictures of Jesus healing the sick, cuddling babies, and comforting friends. Other books describe in graphic detail what happens when people reject God and live as though He doesn't exist. Invading armies plunder and destroy. Famine and disease ravage communities. Conquering kings march captives off to faraway lands to enslave and oppress them.

These books declare what we know but don't like to acknowledge, that our holy and righteous Father doesn't wink at sin. He has unleashed His wrath on those who slander His name and reject His offer of salvation in the past, and He will do it again.

As the writer of Hebrews explained, "If we deliberately keep on sinning after we have received the knowledge of the truth, no sacrifice for sins is left, but only a fearful expectation of judgment and of raging fire that will consume the enemies of God" (Hebrews 10:26–27).

If people reject God and the sacrifice Jesus made on the cross to pay for their sins, they have no hope. "'The Lord will judge his people.' It is a dreadful thing to fall into the hands of the living God" (vv. 30–31).

But what about those of us who sincerely follow God and seek to do His will, yet drift off into sinful disobedience? Or deliberately walk off the path of purity and holiness God calls us to? What hope do we have? Our sins offend the same God who judged nations for their wicked actions and sinful hearts.

I'm grateful God knows our frailties and our propensity to sin. "As a father has compassion on his children," the psalmist wrote, "so the Lord has compassion on those who fear him; for he knows how we are formed, he remembers that we are dust" (Psalm 103:13–14).

Although Christ's death on the cross crucified sin's power to condemn a believer to hell, we'll continue to wrestle with our compulsion to sin until we die. If we think otherwise, 1 John 1:8 warns us, "we deceive ourselves and the truth is not in us."

The apostle Paul described this excruciating struggle in Romans 7. "For I do not do the good I want to do, but the evil I do not want to do—this I keep on doing. Now if I do what I do not want to do, it is no longer I who do it, but it is sin living in me that does it" (vv. 19–20).

What hope do we have when (not if) the sinful nature inside us wins a skirmish?

Listen to the tender words of the apostle John, writing to struggling believers. "My dear children, I write this to you so that you will not sin. But if anybody does sin, we have an advocate with the Father—Jesus Christ, the Righteous One. He is the atoning sacrifice for our sins, and not only for ours but also for the sins of the whole world" (1 John 2:1–2).

When we sin, we can run to Jesus. We can confess our failings to His empathetic ears, and instantly receive His gift of forgiveness. We can know He'll advocate before the Father on our behalf. C. H. Spurgeon once said, "You stand before God as if you were Christ, because Christ stood before God as if He were you."[4]

When Satan accuses us before God, Jesus stands in our defense (Zechariah 3:1–7; Revelation 12:10). When the enemy of our soul waves the putrid garments of our sinful acts and cries, "Guilty," Jesus drapes the snow-white raiment washed in His blood over our sin and cries, "Forgiven."

When we weep before the Father, brokenhearted over our actions and pleading for victory, Jesus intercedes for us as the one who was similarly tempted and yet victorious.

Yes, we will sin. And yes, as the prophets of old warned, our sin offends our holy God. But we needn't lose hope. Instead of fainting in the battle, we can pursue holiness and unhindered fellowship with Him because Jesus, our Champion, is our Advocate.

Take Heart

When a believer sins, Jesus, our Advocate, defends us against our accuser and intercedes for us before our Father.

From the Heart

Oh, Father, some days I'm so disappointed with myself. And I'm so far from holy. Help me remember that even the strongest Christian sins sometimes. Only Jesus made it through this world without sinning. You know my heart—that I want my life to bring you glory, not shame. Help me conduct myself in purity and holiness, but when I fail, remind me of Jesus, who ever lives to make intercession for me. I love you. Amen.

8

God Isn't Limited by Time and Space

**The Lord himself goes before you
and will be with you; he will never
leave you nor forsake you. Do not be
afraid; do not be discouraged.**

DEUTERONOMY 31:8

Nothing has tested my faith more than releasing my children to God.

If you're a parent, you understand. From the moment the doctor places that baby in our arms, we'd give our life to protect them. We watch their little chests rise and fall while they sleep. We research the best crib mattress, car seat, and pediatrician. We buy shin guards when they play soccer, mouth guards when they play football, and helmets when they ride their bikes. Eternal vigilance is our motto, and nothing gets past us.

In my daughters' early years, I had an exalted perception of my ability to protect them. Then they grew up.

They traveled to places I couldn't go and did things I couldn't do. One had the audacity to attend college two states away. The other accepted an internship and then a job in one of the busiest and most dangerous cities in the country. Both traveled *out of the country* on mission trips. How was I supposed to keep them safe?

And then, daughter number one married a naval officer and moved to Japan.

Yokosuka, Japan.

Seven thousand miles away.

To reach her, I'd have to take a fourteen-hour flight that crossed seven time zones and one very large ocean. How on earth could I keep her safe when she lived so far away?

I couldn't.

But God could. Unlike me, He isn't limited by time, space, and international travel law. He doesn't require a passport or a plane ticket. He's nearer to her and more intimately aware of her needs than I ever could be.

Before my daughter left, I tucked a Bible verse into her suitcase. "The LORD himself goes before you and will be with you; he will never leave you nor forsake you. Do not be afraid; do not be discouraged" (Deuteronomy 31:8).

I shared the verse with her, but did I believe it?

Like the father with the sick son in Mark 9:24, I prayed, "Lord, I believe. Help my unbelief." I knew in my head I could trust God with my daughter, but my heart still wavered.

One morning as I drove to work, I replayed the early morning conversation we'd had. Her husband had deployed, and she was terribly lonely. She lived far from base and didn't know anyone. My heart ached for her.

"Lord, you have to help her," I prayed, "because I can't. Please send her a friend."

I continued to think about her as I seated Alexa, my first dental patient. I'd cared for her and her sisters for years. After I asked questions about her dental health, our conversation turned to family news.

"What's Andrea doing these days?" I asked. "I haven't seen her in a while."

"That's because she moved to Japan," Alexa said.

"Japan? What a coincidence. My daughter just moved to Japan. Where does she live?"

She bit her lip, trying to remember the unfamiliar name. "Yo . . . Yo . . . "

"Yokosuka?" I said.

"Yes! That's it."

"That's where my daughter lives. What's Andrea doing there?"

"She's working with a ministry called Cadence International. They minister to service members and their families."

All thoughts of scaling, polishing, and periodontal assessment flew out of my mind. "Oh, my goodness!" I said. "We need to connect them. If I gave you my daughter's email address, would you pass it along to Andrea? She could really use a friend."

She promised she would, but later that night, doubts assaulted me. *She's a busy mother of three little kids. What if she forgets? Or loses the card I gave her with the email address?*

All the hope and faith I had in God's divine appointment vanished. *I'd better do something.*

I took the address Alexa had given me and composed an email.

For good measure, I attached a photo. A picture is worth a thousand words, right? I hit Send and prayed. *Lord, you know what my girl needs more than I do. Meet her needs according to your riches and glory.* I went to bed praying and woke up praying.

To my delight, Andrea had responded to my email. "It's great to hear from you. I can't believe your daughter's in Japan. I'd be glad to reach out to her." My mother heart thumped with joy.

"I'd already planned to invite her to coffee when I opened the picture you sent," her email continued. "Then I realized I'd already met them—at church on base last Sunday."

Tears of joy sprang to my eyes and blurred the words on the screen. *Oh, Lord,* I prayed, *I'm so sorry for doubting you. You promise to go ahead of us wherever we go. You know my girl's needs and already had a plan in place to meet them. You arranged circumstances and people to minister to her. Forgive me for my wimpy faith.*

In the years following that divine appointment, God has continued to go ahead of my girl into ten plus countries, four continents, and many deployments. He's protected and provided for her in ways I never could have arranged or imagined. Although her journey hasn't always been smooth, God has never left her side.

Whenever I'm tempted to fret because my loved ones are out of my reach, I remember they're not out of God's reach. His promises and presence give me hope.

Take Heart

Not limited by time or space, God promises to go ahead of His children into every situation. We can hope in His unwavering presence.

From the Heart

Father, I'm ashamed to admit I struggle to trust you with my loved ones. I care about them so much, but I know you love them more. I can't go everywhere they go, but you can. You promise to go behind them and before them. You won't allow anything into their lives that isn't part of your good plan to draw them closer to yourself. Meet their needs. Protect and provide for them. As I watch you work, increase my faith. In Jesus's name I ask, amen.

9

God Is Our Deliverer

**As for you, because of the blood of
my covenant with you, I will free your
prisoners from the waterless pit. Return
to your fortress, you prisoners of hope.**

ZECHARIAH 9:11-12

Heather Mercer and Dayna Curry knew the dangers of serving in Afghanistan. They were women in a male-dominated society, and they were Christians in a Muslim country—ruled by the Taliban.

But their desire to serve "the least of these" and their love for Christ planted them there anyway. Only twenty-four years old, Heather had simple but lofty goals: "I joined a church planting team that moved to Afghanistan basically to live among the people, to serve them in practical and tangible ways, and then, through relationships, to begin to share Christ."⁵ She and Dayna were doing just that the day they were captured.

A family they'd been ministering to asked about their faith and expressed a desire to watch the *Jesus* film. When the women left their home after showing the film, Taliban soldiers were waiting for them.

"We were interrogated, every day, for about ten hours a day," Heather said. "We didn't know if anyone knew if we were dead or alive. . . . There were moments of real fear, and there were also moments of tremendous peace." People everywhere prayed for their release.

Midway through their trial, the events of September 11, 2001, occurred, thrusting the world into the Global War on Terror, with the Taliban as the prime target.

The trial was suspended, and the women became hostages. Shuttled from one prison to another as Taliban forces moved about the country, Heather and Dayna experienced increasingly deplorable conditions.

They'd just been moved to their fifth prison when the allied forces began their assault. As the United States bombed Taliban strongholds in Ghazni, Taliban members fled. Bombs exploded around the prison as the captives prayed. Christians around the world prayed with them.

After hours of fighting, the girls heard silence for a span of thirty minutes. Then the assault began again, this time against the jail doors. Had the Taliban returned?

As they waited, trembling, they heard footsteps rushing toward their cell. Heather recounted what happened next: "This Rambo-looking Afghan runs into the room yelling, 'You're free! You're free!'"

The captives raced into the city, but fighting drove them back into the prison. Hours later they emerged again and stumbled onto what looked like the Macy's Thanksgiving Day Parade. As they wound through the streets, hundreds of Afghans piled in line in behind them, waving and celebrating their liberation. Heather and Dayna waved back.

"Congratulations, you're free!" they cried.[6] They were free indeed.

Zechariah prophesied to a people who had been similarly imprisoned. Carried off into captivity in Babylon, the Israelites had no hope of deliverance. They'd been vanquished by their enemies and held hostage against their will. But God moved the heart of pagan King Cyrus to free the exiles and allow them to return home. There the word of the Lord came to them, promising deliverance that far surpassed any military victory.

> Rejoice greatly, Daughter Zion!
>   Shout, Daughter Jerusalem!
> See, your king comes to you,
>   righteous and victorious,
> lowly and riding on a donkey,
>   on a colt, the foal of a donkey. . . .
> He will proclaim peace to the nations.
>   His rule will extend from sea to sea
>   and from the River to the ends of the earth.
> As for you, because of the blood of my covenant with you,
>   I will free your prisoners from the waterless pit.
> Return to your fortress, you prisoners of hope. (Zechariah 9:9–12)

Now we know Zechariah's words pointed God's people to an emancipation far greater than the temporary rule of one government over another. His words lifted their eyes to the day when the Messiah would come and free His people from sin, death, and hell for all eternity.

Sadly, Israel missed her deliverer. While they waited for a Rambo-like military leader to break the yoke of Rome and set up his earthly kingdom, they rejected the God-man who offered His life on a cross to usher in His heavenly kingdom.

We who have believed, however, have hope. We know, like Heather and Dayna, that whether we're imprisoned or free, shackled or unfettered, we possess a freedom that surpasses anything mankind can offer.

This freedom guarantees sin cannot master us, hell cannot threaten us, and death cannot hold us. The Deliverer of all deliverers has vanquished our enemies and leads us in triumphant procession shouting, "Congratulations, you're free!"

"So if the Son sets you free, you will be free indeed" (John 8:36).

Take Heart

When we walk in light of what Christ has accomplished for us, we can live faith-filled, fearless, and hopeful lives for God's glory.

From the Heart

Thank you, oh, thank you, dear Father, for breaking the chains of sin, death, and hell and setting us free. Help me walk every day in the freedom you purchased on the cross. When I battle sin, remind me that you've already won the fight and have given me everything I need to live a godly life. When the fear of death disturbs my peace, keep my mind centered on you and the hope of heaven. Remind me that death is simply the portal to eternity. Help me never forget that the only One who holds me captive is you. Because of Christ, I can live as a prisoner of hope. In the mighty name of Jesus I ask, amen.

10

God Never Forgets

**Can a mother forget the baby at
her breast and have no compassion on
the child she has borne? Though she
may forget, I will not forget you!**

ISAIAH 49:15

One of my secret fears as a soon-to-be mother was that I'd walk off and forget I had a baby. What if a friend called with a spur-of-the-moment invitation, and I grabbed my purse and car keys and headed out the door, leaving my infant daughter sleeping in her crib? Or got sucked into the latest sitcom and binge-watched for hours, totally forgetting my baby strapped in her swing in the kitchen?

Once my daughter was born, I learned how improbable that fear was. From the moment the doctor laid my tiny babe in my arms, we were forever linked. He may have cut the cord that separated her body from mine, but nothing could sever the all-consuming awareness that I had a child—a precious, beautiful, made-in-God's-image child.

First, my body reminded me. Every two to three hours, I experienced an increasingly urgent desire to nurse her. Whenever I laughed or (heaven help me) sneezed, the stitches from my C-section that held my belly closed reminded me a child had been plucked from my womb. And after the stitches resorbed and the tape peeled off, a scar remained—a permanent testimony that her life had begun within mine.

As physical manifestations resolved, psychological ones took their place. I'd rise in the night, even before my child cried, to make sure she was warm, dry, and still breathing. When I left her with a sitter (Grandma only) for a doctor's appointment or a quick trip to the store, I'd leave behind a list of instructions and call twice to check in. Sometimes I cut short the outing because I missed her. My desire to be near her and know she was safe was so strong I'd usually bring her along, even if it was awkward or inconvenient. The emotional angst just wasn't worth it.

Forget my child? Never.

Perhaps this permanent love bond hardwired into a woman's DNA is why God used the example of a mother to reassure the Israelites (and believers down through the ages) that He, their heavenly parent, would never forget them.

As trials increased and God seemed far away, the Israelites wondered. They voiced their fears aloud. "The LORD has forsaken me," Isaiah wrote, "the Lord has forgotten me" (Isaiah 49:14).

We shake our heads at the foolishness of the Israelites. How could they doubt God's love when He had so clearly displayed it for the world to see? When history testified of centuries of His unwavering care? Their own scrolls bore witness to God's never-ending faithfulness.

He called Abraham out of a pagan country and made a great nation of him. He preserved Jacob, his twelve sons, and their families during a nationwide famine. He sheltered the Israelites in Egypt, then emancipated them from the strongest country in the world. When they turned their faithless faces away from Him in the desert, He continued to feed, clothe, and guide them. Then He brought them into the promised land—just as He had sworn to Abraham centuries before.

We shake our heads at Israel's doubt, yet we so easily fall into the same fearful questioning.

When death robs us of a loved one, we wonder if God has turned a deaf ear to our prayers. When our hearts bleed from the wounds of a prodigal child, we question God's power to save. When financial, family, or health difficulties make us fear the future, we doubt God's care.

When the trials of this life stretch before us in a never-ending parade that looks more like a funeral procession, we join the Israelites and wonder if we have left God's notice. Whether we shriek the words in lament or whisper them into our tear-soaked pillows, God hears our cries and answers us.

"Can a mother forget the baby at her breast and have no compassion on the child she has borne? Though she may forget, I will not forget you!" (Isaiah 49:15).

Then, as Jesus did with doubting Thomas, He stretches out His nail-scarred hands and offers irrefutable proof of His love: "See, I have engraved you on the palms of my hands" (v. 16).

When we wonder, in our trials, if God has forgotten us, we need look no further than the nails and the cross.

God will not forsake us. He will not forget us. We are His children forever.

He has engraved us on the palms of His hands.

In this we can find hope.

Take Heart

Jesus's nail-scarred hands testify for all eternity that He will never forget us.

From the Heart

Father, strengthen my fearful and hopeless heart. When I'm tempted to doubt or wonder if you've forgotten me, lift my eyes to the cross. Help me picture your nail-pierced hands cradling me, protecting me, interceding for me, and loving me. "Lord, I believe. Help my unbelief" (Mark 9:24).

11

God
Knows Everything

**Oh, the depth of the riches
of the wisdom and knowledge of God!**

ROMANS 11:33

One of the reasons I enjoy spending time with my grandchildren is because they help me feel smart. Especially four-year-old Andrew. With rare exception, I can answer any question he asks.

"Gigi, why does it get dark at night?"

"Gigi, why do we burp?"

"Gigi, how do snakes move if they have no legs?" (I had to look this one up.)

When I homeschooled my high school daughters, I got the answers to their questions right about half the time. The closer they got to college graduation, the wider my knowledge gap grew. Now in their respective fields, they know far more than I do about many subjects.

Then there's my business major son-in-law who coordinates shipping operations to provide raw material to vital industries. And my naval officer aeronautical engineer son-in-law who can calculate the speed and trajectory of a missile designed to knock another missile out of space. They kindly indulge me with simplified explanations of what they do, but I'm smart enough to realize I could never hold my own in an in-depth conversation.

I don't feel offended that they know more than I do in their areas of expertise. I certainly don't attempt to advise them, offer suggestions, or tell them how to do their jobs. I'm glad smart people use their insight and education to benefit others and make our world a better place. I'm comfortable with what I don't know.

I wonder if Job felt this way when he and God had a heart-to-heart talk.

You know Job's story. Despite God himself declaring Job was "blameless and upright" (Job 1:1), He allowed a string of horrific tragedies to swoop into Job's life. In a single day, he lost his fortune and his children. Soon after, he lost his health. All he had left was a grieving wife who suggested he curse God and die and three questionable friends.

Almost all the forty-two chapters of Job record conversations between him and his friends. Convinced God must be punishing him for some secret sin, they interrogated him and urged him to confess and repent. Job held fast to his integrity and insisted he was innocent.

Like most of us when we suffer, Job questioned God. "If I have sinned, what have I done to you, you who see everything we do? Why have you made me your target? Have I become a burden to you?" (Job 7:20).

As his suffering continued, Job grew bolder. "I desire to speak to the Almighty," he told his friends, "and to argue my case with God" (Job 13:3).

Anyone who has suffered loss understands Job's desire to know why. To make sense of the senseless and ask the hard questions. *Why me? Why now? What have I done to deserve this?*

It doesn't take long for our questions to shift toward God. *God, you control everything. You could have prevented this, yet you allowed it. Why? Are you cruel? Absent? Don't you care?*

God, in His mercy, responded to Job's questions, but not the way he anticipated.

"Then the LORD spoke to Job out of the storm. He said: 'Who is this that obscures my plans with words without knowledge? Brace yourself like a man; I will question you, and you shall answer me'" (Job 38:1–3).

And boy, did He question him. At least sixty-six times. Here's a sample: "Where were you when I laid the earth's foundation? Tell me, if you understand. Who marked off its dimensions? Surely you know! Who stretched a measuring line across it? On what were its footings set, or who laid its cornerstone?" (Job 38:4–6).

The questions came faster than Job could process them. "Can you call forth the rain? Can you send out the lightning? Can you count the clouds?" At the end of their one-sided conversation, Job came up with only one answer—*the* answer.

"I know that you can do all things; no purpose of yours can be thwarted. You asked, 'Who is this that obscures my plans without knowledge?' Surely I spoke of things I did not understand, things too wonderful for me to know. . . . My ears had heard of you but now my eyes have seen you. Therefore I despise myself and repent in dust and ashes" (Job 42:2–3, 5–6).

God, in His infinite kindness, chose to answer Job's questions with questions of His own—questions designed to reveal Job's ignorance and God's infinite knowledge. He didn't question Job as a harsh critic, but as a kind Father. He sought to teach Job about himself and grow his perspective of God. At the end of God's questions, Job realized, as I did when faced with the superior knowledge of my family members, that our understanding is severely limited.

A proper perspective of ourselves and of God is a gift—one that bolsters our hope and trust. When we realize how limited our wisdom and perspective are and how vast God's are, how can we not trust Him?

It makes sense to trust the One who laid the earth's foundation and hung the stars in place. To put our faith in the Creator who fills heaven's storehouses with hail and snow. To surrender to the all-wise God who set limits for the seas and commands the morning.

God never told Job the reason for his pain or explained the purpose of his suffering. Instead, as *The MacArthur Daily Bible* states, "He asked Job if he was as eternal, great, powerful, wise, and perfect as God. If not, Job would have been better off to be quiet and trust Him."[7]

Like Job, we can have confident hope that God will order our days in wisdom and love. We don't have to understand. We just have to trust.

Take Heart

When our world crashes in, God's superior wisdom gives us confident hope and an unshakable reason to trust Him.

From the Heart

Father, thank you for being so far above human wisdom and understanding that I can't help but trust you. When I don't understand what you're doing, strengthen my faith. When my heart breaks at an outcome you allow but I don't like, help me hope in your wisdom. Remind me of your ongoing love and care for me, even when I don't understand my situation or circumstances. When I'm struggling, use Job's story to remind me of how I can trust you to bring beauty from ashes. Amen.

12

God of Never-Ending Love

**But when the kindness and love of
God our Savior appeared, he saved us,
not because of righteous things we had
done, but because of his mercy.**

TITUS 3:4-5

A week before my eighth birthday, I noticed an itchy bump on my belly. The next morning, I found another on my face and two on my arm. By the end of the day, Itchy Bump number 1 and its three friends had multiplied into an army of sores that covered every inch of my body. When I looked into the mirror the following day, I burst into tears. "I'm so ugly," I wailed.

Mom opened her arms and drew my itchy, oozy self into her warm embrace.

"You're not ugly," she said. "I love you."

Every now and then, I have a flashback to my eight-year-old self. Only instead of looking into the bathroom mirror, I look into the mirror of my heart—the one that reflects the deepest part of me— and I burst into tears. I caught the disease of chicken pox from a third-grade classmate, but I inherited the disease of sin from my fore-father Adam.

Sometimes memories of my past life, before Christ, drag my thoughts to the years when I totally disregarded God and His ways. I cared nothing about serving Him, only myself. I pursued what I thought would make me happy, fulfilled, and successful. I lived independent of God, and I liked it that way. Compared to God's holiness and purity, I was a scabby, oozy mess—only I didn't know it.

Titus 3 puts it like this: "At one time we too were foolish, disobedient, deceived and enslaved by all kinds of passions and pleasures. We lived in malice and envy, being hated and hating one another" (v. 3).

Then I heard God's Word preached and taught, and a curious thing happened. The mirror of God's Word revealed my sin, and I could see it for what it was—ugly and offensive to a holy God.

But instead of turning away from me in disgust, God the Father opened His arms and drew me into His embrace.

"You're not ugly," He said. "I love you."

"But when the kindness and love of God our Savior appeared, he saved us, not because of righteous things we had done, but because of his mercy. He saved us through the washing of rebirth and renewal by the Holy Spirit, whom he poured out on us generously through Jesus Christ our Savior" (vv. 4–6).

God cleansed me from my sin and made me beautiful in His eyes.

I wish the ugliness of sin disappeared when I accepted Christ as my Savior. I long for the day when I'll no longer wrestle with it. Selfish actions, unkind words, willful disobedience rise up in me more often than I care to admit. Christ won the victory over sin on the cross, but I continue to struggle with it in this lifetime.

Until I die, I'll win battles and lose battles. Some days I'll walk faithfully and full of joy. Other days I'll stumble and come to Him in sorrow. I'll weep over my sin and wonder if He grows tired of the ugliness of my failures.

But God's Word reminds me that whether I come to Him ten times or a hundred, He'll open His arms, draw me close, and whisper in my ear, "You're not ugly. I love you."

Take Heart

When we grow discouraged by our imperfections and spiritual immaturity, the comfort of God's never-ending love gives us hope.

From the Heart

Father, I want to please you with my life, but sometimes I fail miserably. I give in to old habits, act selfishly, and avoid doing what I know is best. The past condemns me and tries to convince me there's no way you could love me. Remind me every day of your never-ending love. Thank you for knowing my weaknesses and loving me anyway.

13

God of All Comfort

**He was despised and rejected by men, a
man of sorrows and acquainted with grief.**

ISAIAH 53:3 ESV

I sat alone in my quiet time spot with my Bible on my lap. Not praying. Not reading. Just sitting. Somehow, feeling my Bible's comforting weight and well-worn cover brought me peace.

We'd buried my beloved grandmother earlier that day. The granny who taught me to say the Twenty-Third Psalm lying in bed next to her as she said her prayers. The one who gave me dollar bills from her shiny black purse and sent me off to the store to buy treats. The one who tried—several times—to teach me to crochet.

Granny's apartment smelled like cabbage, old books, and coffee. And, sometimes, like Portuguese doughnuts. She kept a two-liter bottle of Sprite and a package of chocolate chip cookies in her pantry—just in case company stopped by. She liked her instant coffee dark and her cake slices thick.

We received friends after the small graveside service, and their words of comfort filtered through my mind. I kept returning to one friend's words.

"She lived a long time," she said. "But you know, death is a part of life."

Death is a part of life. While I knew these words were true, they didn't settle well on my aching heart. Should we accept death simply because it is a part of life?

I remembered another funeral scene. Mary and Martha weeping for days for their beloved brother, Lazarus. Wondering why Jesus had allowed their brother—His friend—to die.

"Lord," Martha had cried when He finally arrived, "if you had been here, my brother would not have died" (John 11:21). Mary made the same accusation, lamenting the loss of life and the sucker punch of grief (v. 32).

Standing outside the tomb beside those heartbroken sisters, Jesus wept.

Have you ever wondered why?

Jesus knew He was about to do one of the greatest miracles of His ministry. With three words from Jesus's holy lips, Lazarus would spring to life, and everyone's grief would be banished. The funeral would become a celebration, and tears of sorrow would become tears of joy. Why then did Jesus weep?

I believe He wept for what could have been. He created us to live forever in a world untouched by disease, pain, and death. But when

Adam and Eve sinned, they opened the gate to the garden and invited death into God's perfect world. They corrupted His perfect design. "The wages of sin is death," Romans 6:23 declares. Humankind has collected these wages for millennia.

Surrounded by His weeping friends and touched by their grief, Jesus was heartbroken. While He knew what they didn't—that He was preparing to conquer death, first in Lazarus and then forever on the cross—His Spirit still agonized with their sorrows. Isaiah 53:3 describes Him as "a man of sorrows and acquainted with grief" (ESV). Even today, He grieves with us as we mourn the loss of beloved grandmothers, parents, children, and friends.

One day, one glorious day, physical and spiritual death will be banished. When Christ has dismantled Satan's rule, authority, and power over the earth, Jesus will reign "until he has put all his enemies under his feet. The last enemy to be destroyed is death" (1 Corinthians 15:25–26).

Then "death and Hades [will be] thrown into the lake of fire" (Revelation 20:14).

Glory hallelujah!

"He will wipe every tear from [our] eyes. There will be no more death or mourning or crying or pain" (Revelation 21:4).

When death takes another loved one from my life, I take comfort in knowing Jesus grieves with me and offers comfort only He can give.

Take Heart

Because Jesus is our Savior, we never grieve alone.

From the Heart

Jesus, I know you broke the power of sin and death at the cross, but it's easy to lose sight of this victory because people still die—people I love. Thank you for walking beside me when the shadow of death touches my life. Thank you for surrounding me with your arms of love and compassion and weeping with me. Knowing that you're The Man of Sorrows who weeps with me helps me feel less alone. Thank you for defeating death and promising to banish it forever. The hope you promised of a forever future with no mourning, crying, or pain helps me go on. In the tender name of Jesus I pray, amen.

14

God of Wisdom

If any of you lacks wisdom, you should ask God, who gives generously to all without finding fault, and it will be given to you.

JAMES 1:5

I suspect if someone asked, "Who'd like to be mature and complete in your faith?" most of us would wave our hands wildly and yell, "I do! I do!"

But when we discover the route to maturity winds through the wilderness of trial? "Uh, no. Never mind. Maturity's overrated."

Trials are especially good at revealing areas of spiritual immaturity and our need for godly wisdom. During my daughter's turbulent adolescent years, I found myself on my face before the Lord crying out for wisdom almost every day. Challenging patches in my marriage motivate me to seek wise counsel and resources. And when times of conflict threaten our ministry, we pray, fast, and seek God's will about how to proceed.

Almost forty years into this Christian life of mine, I still need to be reminded that God freely offers me His wisdom.

"If any of you lacks wisdom," James wrote, "you should ask God, who gives generously to all without finding fault, and it will be given to you" (1:5).

It's no coincidence that James declared God's glorious, hope-filled promise smack-dab in the middle of a life-is-hard-but-God-is-good pep talk to the Jews scattered abroad because of persecution.

"Consider it pure joy, my brothers and sisters, whenever you face trials of many kinds, because you know that the testing of your faith produces perseverance. Let perseverance finish its work so that you may be mature and complete, not lacking anything" (James 1:2–4).

I tend to look at trials as bad, and they would be apart from God's sovereign purposes. From God's perspective, however, trials enter our lives only with His permission—and only to accomplish His will. Part of His will is that we persevere, mature, and seek His wisdom.

These aspects of trials can bring deep and abiding joy. But first they bring pain, and we don't get to opt out. "In the world," Jesus warned, "you will have tribulation" (John 16:33 ESV).

But we do get to choose how we respond to trials. We can seek God's wisdom, or we can attempt to figure them out ourselves.

Before I had a relationship with Christ, I'd tackle trials with everything I had. It never occurred to me to ask God for insight or direction. Sometimes I fall back into this mindset. I leave God out of the equation until I'm desperate. Only when I've exhausted all my wisdom and resources do I cry out to God.

James, the brother of the Lord, suggests another way—a better way. Ask God for wisdom. Then believe what He tells you (James 1:5–6).

Knowing God promises a sure and steady source of wisdom for times of trial gives me the hope I need to persevere.

But what does God's wisdom look like? And where do we find it?

The first and most obvious source is the Bible. But we can't just throw open its cover like an emergency tool kit, fumble around until we find something that looks like it might work, and duct tape it to the problem. We gain God's wisdom through a sincere and diligent search.

Proverbs 2:1–5 describes it this way:

> My son, if you accept my words and store up my commands within you, turning your ear to wisdom and applying your heart to understanding—indeed, if you call out for insight and cry aloud for understanding, and if you look for it as for silver and search for it as for hidden treasure, then you will understand the fear of the LORD and find the knowledge of God.

A second source of God's wisdom comes through prayer. I discovered that if I bathe my Bible reading in prayer, God often speaks to me through my reading for the day. He also speaks through sermons and biblical messages, and the voice of His Spirit in my heart. Sometimes I forget to listen and spend all my time talking. "God, you've got to fix this. Lord, show me what to do. Father, I'm so confused, frustrated, anxious, upset." But when I embrace the words of Psalm 46:10, "Be still, and know that I am God," my heart quiets, and I can hear God speak.

Often God will impart His wisdom through the counsel of others. But we must choose our sources carefully. Rather than blab my problems to everyone who will listen, I've learned to seek out those who are grounded in God's Word, mature in their faith, and wise in their experience. I've also learned there's no shame in seeking help. Proverbs 11:14, written by Solomon, the wisest man who ever lived, reminds us, "Where there is no counsel, the people fall: but in the multitude of counselors there is safety" (NKJV).

Everyone, believers and unbelievers, encounter trials. The glorious hope we have as Christians is that God offers us His wisdom freely and without reproach. All we have to do is ask.

Take Heart

God's supernatural wisdom is only one prayer away.

From the Heart

Forgive me, Father, for being so quick to tackle my problems in my own strength, with my own wisdom, and totally ignoring you. Or waiting until the situation is so desperate I have nowhere else to turn. Thank you for the reminder of James 1:5 and the promise that you'll give me insight and direction every time I ask. Teach me to come to you first, not last, every time I need wisdom. In Jesus's name I ask, amen.

15

God Is Trustworthy

As for God, his way is perfect.

PSALM 18:30

Something unsettling happened after I surrendered my life to Christ.

Along with the assurance that I'd spend eternity with God when I died came a new realization. A terrifying realization.

I understood that the same truths that applied to me and my eternal destiny applied to my loved ones as well. If they died without accepting Christ as their Savior, they'd spend eternity separated from God.

My parents. My sisters. My friends. My beloved grandmother.

Each person would stand before God and give an account for what they had done with Jesus. Had they accepted Him or rejected Him? John 3:17–18 explained, "For God did not send his Son into the world to condemn the world, but to save the world through him. Whoever believes in him is not condemned, but whoever does not believe stands condemned already because they have not believed in the name of God's one and only Son."

This realization compelled me to share the simple truths of the gospel with everyone I cared about. I began with my immediate family. One by one I told them what I'd learned (to read a simple explanation of the gospel, turn to page 263).

When I did, God opened Mom's heart to believe and place her faith in Christ. Dad shared how he'd surrendered his life to Jesus as a boy at a Billy Graham crusade. One sister prayed to receive Christ at a Christian concert. Over a period of years, I had the opportunity to share my faith with many loved ones and friends. Most listened. Some responded.

But then there was the matter of my beloved Rhode Island granny. By now our family lived a thousand miles away in South Carolina. I couldn't just pop in and share the gospel with her. Email and Face-Time hadn't happened yet, so those options weren't available. But I could write letters.

And write I did. First, I shared my salvation experience, complete with Bible verses. In subsequent letters, I sprinkled biblical breadcrumbs among the family updates. I'd tell her what I was learning about God, myself, and the world. The first time we visited, my new husband and I shared our faith stories.

God granted me many years and many opportunities to share and live out my faith before my granny. To my knowledge, she never bowed her head and prayed a formal prayer of salvation, but God knows what's in her heart. All it takes is surrender and simple faith. I have hope that I'll see her one day in heaven.

First, I can have hope for Granny's salvation because of how God saved me. Despite my lack of interest in spiritual things, He softened my heart. He could soften Granny's heart, too. I loved her tremendously, but He loved her enough to die for her.

Second, since the beginning of time, God has been reconciling lost men and women to himself. They don't seek Him. He seeks them. He pursues them, awakens them, forgives them, and welcomes them into His family. He continues to do this today.

Third, God placed her in my family. Although no one is saved by virtue of another family member's faith, He orchestrated that she heard the gospel through me. She witnessed how God transformed my life. She was the object of a thousand of my prayers. This didn't happen by accident. It was by God's design to accomplish His good purposes in her life.

Even if I hadn't had a chance to share my faith with Granny, I could still rest in hope for her salvation because God reveals himself through other believers. Perhaps a kind caregiver shared her faith. Or a neighbor. Or the woman who delivered her Meals-on-Wheels dinners.

We often mistakenly assume that our loved ones' salvation is all up to us. While we should avail ourselves of every opportunity to witness, we must also realize He places other believers in our loved ones' lives. He uses them in ways we could never orchestrate to impact them.

I also have hope for her salvation because God reveals himself to everyone through His creation. Romans 1:20 tells us, "For since the creation of the world God's invisible qualities—his eternal power and divine nature—have been clearly seen, being understood from what has been made." All her life, creation testified to her about its Creator. If she responded to what she saw, God was pleased to reveal more of himself to her.

Finally, I can rest in biblical hope because God's Word never returns void. It always accomplishes what God intends (Isaiah 55:11). I can be confident that the Bible verses my grandmother read and heard did what God intended them to do. God used them to reveal her sin and her need for a Savior. God assures us, "Everyone who calls on the name of the Lord will be saved" (Romans 10:13). If Granny called upon God, I can have sure and certain hope she was saved.

I won't know until I get to heaven if my Granny is there, but I can rest in hope based on the nature and character of God. Psalm 18:30 reassures us, "As for God, his way is perfect." I can trust God with those I love.

Take Heart

We may not fully understand God and His matchless character, but we can fully trust Him with our unsaved loved ones. We can rest in hope.

From the Heart

Father, I'm comforted to know that you make no mistakes. You do all things well. You're worthy of my trust and worship. Thank you for being wise, just, compassionate, longsuffering, and gracious. Your character assures me I can fully trust you with my unsaved loved ones. Thank you for orchestrating the events of their lives to reveal yourself to them. Whenever I'm tempted to fret, help me pray and trust you instead. Give me boldness and opportunities to share the gospel with them, then trust you to do immeasurably more than I can ever ask or imagine. Save them, I pray, amen.

16

God Is Generous

**No good thing does he withhold
from those who walk uprightly.**

PSALM 84:11 ESV

On the wall in our home hangs a shadow box. You've seen the type—a wooden box with a glass front and compartments to hold curios or memorabilia. Unlike most shadow boxes that contain service medals or other collectables, ours showcases items that symbolize dramatic acts God has done in our family's life.

One compartment holds a rock from the wall my husband sat on when he gave his life to Christ. Another houses a canceled bill from the hospital where our second daughter was born declaring that our debt had been forgiven. The top left square displays a tiny desktop computer.

The toy computer joined our collection in the thirteenth year of our marriage. It's a replica of our first well-loved computer. The one that died a sudden and dreadful death.

We all agreed that our computer couldn't have picked a worse time to breathe its last. My husband was in the middle of updating his résumé for a job search. Both daughters had school assignments. I had a homeschool support group to run.

And then there was the rather obvious fact that our emergency fund didn't have hundreds of dollars in it to buy a new computer. David worked hard, and his job supplied for our needs, but there wasn't much left over at the end of each month. Because we home-schooled, I worked only a few afternoons a week. If God didn't supply a computer, we had no other options.

Our girls were old enough to understand broken computers, empty bank accounts, and prayer, so we included them in the discussion over dinner the day the computer went to cyber heaven.

"God promises in His Word, 'No good thing does he withhold from those who walk uprightly'" (Psalm 84:11 ESV). I shared a quote from a book I'd been reading. "Thomas Watson, the old Puritan preacher, said, 'If it is good for us, we shall have it; if it is not good for us, then the withholding of it is good.'[8]

"Let's pray and ask God to provide another computer if it will be good for us," I said. We bowed our heads and petitioned God as eloquently as we knew how. My prayer included a bullet-point list of why a computer was a *need* in our household, not just a *want*.

When we opened our eyes, there sat our old computer, still deader than dead. When the kids weren't looking, I punched the power button—just in case—but no light flickered. I don't know what I expected. A cyber resurrection, maybe? But God chose not to raise the dead that day.

Three days passed. No unexpected rebate check appeared in our mailbox. No television ads promised bargain-basement prices on electronics. Even though I checked our savings account twice, no unexplained windfall appeared.

"I'm going to call Jim at the church," David said. "He knows a lot about computers. Maybe he can take a look at our computer and see if it's fixable."

When Jim called back a few days later, I held my breath, waiting for the verdict.

"I'm afraid I have bad news," he said. "The motherboard is fried. It doesn't make sense to repair a machine this old."

I released my breath in a disappointed sigh. *Oh well*, I thought. *God can supply a computer some other way.*

I tuned back into the conversation just in time to hear him say, "But I also have some good news. The church just bought new computers for the office, and they asked me to find a school or tutoring center that could use the old ones. They work fine, just not as fast as we'd like. Since you use your computer to homeschool, you guys fit the bill. I can drop one by on my way home from work today and help you set it up."

Jim probably said a few more things before he hung up, but my mind left the pedantic details of CPUs and modem cables and soared into the heavenly realms of praise and thanksgiving.

Yes! my spirit shouted. *You did it, God. You said you'd supply our needs, and you kept your word. Best of all, you showed our girls that we can come to you with legitimate needs, and you will hear and answer our prayers. Thank you, thank you, thank you!*

In the years since, I've asked God for many things. Some were more wants than needs, yet God graciously supplied much of what I asked for. He's a kind Father who loves to give good gifts to His children.

I've prayed for true needs, too—healing, rescue from hard situations, or financial provision. These requests are huge compared to a broken computer. God has said yes to some of my prayers and no to others. As I've wrestled through the mystery of God's ways, I often reflect on a conversation I had with a wise Bible teacher.

A woman in our study had requested prayer for a young mother gravely ill in a nearby hospital.

"I know God's going to heal her," the woman said. "She has two little girls, and they need their mother."

"God promises to supply our needs," our teacher said, "but only He knows what our greatest needs are. I pray with all my heart that God will heal her. But if the Lord chooses to take her home, we can trust that He knows something we don't about what's ultimately best."

God's promise to meet our needs, paired with His infinite wisdom about what our truest and deepest needs are, give me hope to weather even the most challenging times. They give me boldness to ask freely, trust wholeheartedly, and lay my whys at His feet.

Take Heart

As we seek to walk in God's ways, we can rest in the confidence that we will lack nothing He, in His infinite wisdom, knows we need.

From the Heart

Thank you, Father, for promising to withhold nothing good from us. Help me remember to bring all my needs—big ones, small ones, and some I'm not even sure are needs—to you in prayer. Grow my faith as I see you provide. Grow my trust when the answer is long in coming or different from what I asked. Help me rest in the knowledge that you who know me better than I know myself have a perfect understanding of what I need. Use the yeses and the noes to draw me closer to yourself. In Jesus's precious name I pray, amen.

17

God Alone
Reigns Supreme

> LORD, the God of our ancestors, are you
> not the God who is in heaven? You rule
> over all the kingdoms of the nations.
> Power and might are in your hand,
> and no one can withstand you.

2 CHRONICLES 20:6

Do you remember the first time you voted? I do. I felt heady with power as I clutched my voter registration card and made my way to the polls. My vote, I was convinced, would change the world.

I'd become a Christian two years earlier, and my politics had altered considerably. Now I was prepared to cast a vote for righteousness as I ticked off the boxes and lent my amen to godly candidates with moral agendas. Together with other like-minded voters, we were going to reclaim our country for God.

Much has changed since my first election, but much has stayed the same. I still seek godly candidates with moral agendas, but voting isn't the primary way I try to change the world.

In more than thirty years of voting, I've learned that godly elected officials can inspire hope and optimism for our country. Ungodly ones can cause Christians to experience deep feelings of hopelessness and fear. Thankfully, we have a source of hope that remains stalwart regardless of who's in the White House, governor's mansion, or county council chambers.

If you're struggling with feelings of hopelessness regarding our elected officials, I'd like to share truths that have helped bolster my heart.

God's plans always prevail.

The psalmist declared, "But the plans of the Lord stand firm forever, the purposes of his heart through all generations" (Psalm 33:11). Remembering that God's plans are higher and loftier than what we see in front of us helps us retain our hope when ungodly leaders govern our world. We must never forget God is on a relentless quest to reconcile our lost world to himself and assemble a family of believers that transcends time, geography, and political parties. He uses our leaders to accomplish His purposes. No plan of His can be thwarted.

In obedience to God, we vote, but God ultimately appoints our leaders.

Daniel, one of the godliest men in the Bible, served under five pagan kings. The evil Nebuchadnezzar, who conquered Israel and carted its citizens off to Babylon. Evil-merodach, whose name says it all. Belshazzar, who used implements from the temple to hold drunken parties; Darius, who threw Daniel into the lions' den for praying to someone other than himself; and Cyrus the Great.

Despite working for the most powerful men in the world, Daniel wrote, under inspiration from the Holy Spirit, "Praise be to the name of God for ever and ever; wisdom and power are his. He changes times and seasons; he deposes kings and raises up others" (Daniel 2:20–21).

Every ounce of power our leaders possess has been given to them by God.

Jesus, facing the man who thought he held Jesus's life in his hands, declared the source of ultimate power. During Jesus's trial, Pilate said to Him, "Do you refuse to speak to me? . . . Don't you realize I have power either to free you or to crucify you?"

"Jesus answered, 'You would have no power over me if it were not given to you from above'" (John 19:10–11).

Nothing happens in this world without filtering through God's sovereign hands for His divine purposes, even the crucifixion of His Son. "In the LORD's hand the king's heart is a stream of water that he channels toward all who please him" (Proverbs 21:1).

God, not man, is the sovereign Ruler over nations and kingdoms.

Solomon rightly proclaimed, "LORD, the God of our ancestors, are you not the God who is in heaven? You rule over all the kingdoms of the nations. Power and might are in your hand, and no one can withstand you" (2 Chronicles 20:6).

God's kingdom stands above America and every nation of the earth. When our nations are shaken and the foundations shift, Christ's kingdom remains immovable.

The writer of Hebrews reminded persecuted Jews that they were citizens of a far greater kingdom than Israel. "Therefore, since we are receiving a kingdom that cannot be shaken, let us be thankful, and so worship God acceptably with reverence and awe" (Hebrews 12:28).

God's kingdom will not only withstand attacks from ungodly leaders; it will triumph.

From Cyrus, the Babylonian king of the exile, to the baby-killing Herod, and the Christian-killing Nero, Christianity has never been bested, because our King's power is not from this world. The church Christ birthed when He rose from the dead doesn't depend on qualified human leaders for its success.

"My kingdom is not of this world," Jesus told His disciples on the eve of His crucifixion. "If it were, my servants would fight to prevent my arrest by the Jewish leaders. But now my kingdom is from another place" (John 18:36).

Leaders come and leaders go. Governments rise and fall. Only God, His Word, and people live forever—and we *will* live forever.

"Of the greatness of his government and peace there will be no end. He will reign on David's throne and over his kingdom, establishing and upholding it with justice and righteousness from that time on and forever" (Isaiah 9:7).

We can trust that God is fully in control. He will use all things, even leaders we don't want, for our good and His glory. One day soon, we'll exchange our voter registration card for a passport, one that will take us to a new country, a better country, a country where every knee will bow and every tongue will confess that Jesus Christ is Lord, to the glory of God the Father.

This, my friends, gives us great hope.

Take Heart

God, not human rulers, reigns supreme over the affairs of this world.

From the Heart

Oh, Father, it's so hard not to put my trust in our leaders. And when our leaders fail us again and again, I find it easy to lose hope. Thank you for filling your Word with promises and examples of how you not only accomplished your will despite *ungodly leaders, you did it* because *of them. Remind me that you alone reign supreme. In this I can find great hope.*

God of Covenant Love

**Know therefore that the LORD
your God is God; he is the faithful God,
keeping his covenant of love to a
thousand generations of those who love
him and keep his commandments.**

DEUTERONOMY 7:9

Years had passed since my husband, David, and I had seen Annie, so we were delighted when we ran into her at a local restaurant. Annie and her husband, Javier, led the children's ministry at the first church we attended.

Although dramatically different in personality and giftedness, they made a great team. Javier's huge smile and gregarious nature enabled him to connect easily with children and parents. Annie's quiet spirit provided a soothing counterbalance. He worked up front, and she handled the details.

Now, thirty years later, Annie's golden hair shimmered with silver. Her petite frame carried a few extra pounds, but her smile was timeless.

We hugged, chattered, and hugged again. Swapping phones, we showed off pictures of children and grandchildren.

"How's Javier?" David asked. "Is he here with you?"

Only then did Annie's bright smile dim.

"Javier developed small cell lung cancer," she said. "We lost him about three years ago."

The server called our name, and Annie turned to go, but not before we expressed our condolences and exchanged phone numbers and one more hug. Later, when we met for coffee, she shared the rest of the story.

"Javier struggled a lot," Annie said, choosing her words carefully. "When Sarah was about eight, he decided he didn't want to live with us anymore. He packed his stuff and moved out. I heard through friends he was seeing someone he met at the gym."

She raised her eyes, then lowered them again, tracing the rim of her coffee cup. "We didn't hear from him for years. No visits to see Sarah. No phone calls. No child support. Friends would see him around town, sometimes with a woman, and other times by himself."

Annie took a sip from her cup, then set it down. "Everyone said I should divorce him. I had biblical grounds. But I couldn't. I'd made a promise before God.

"I didn't hear from him again until after his cancer diagnosis." She tore open a sugar packet and emptied it into her mug. "He'd been through chemo and radiation, but the cancer had spread. He wasn't going to make it."

She lifted her eyes to meet mine. "He asked if he could come home. I said yes."

Tears shimmered in the corners of her eyes, and one escaped, making a silver trail from her cheekbone to the angle of her jaw. "He lived nine months. Most of it in a hospital bed we set up in the living room."

I thought of Annie and Javier recently when I read Deuteronomy 7:9. Although, by God's merciful grace, I've not committed sins like Javier, I feel like I fail God in some way every day. On particularly bad days, I grow hopeless. Frustrated with my failures and inconsistencies, I wonder why God doesn't give up on me.

Then I think of Annie.

More than almost anyone I know, she serves as a shining example of God's covenantal love toward His children—toward me and toward you.

Through the patriarch Abraham, and later his descendants, God committed to build a spiritual dynasty that would last forever. Everyone who has ever placed their faith in Him has been grafted into this binding and never-ending marriage covenant. In the covenant God made with Abraham and Israel, He made promises that extend to us.

Listen to Moses's words to the Israelites as they stood poised to enter the promised land: "Know therefore that the LORD your God is God; he is the faithful God, keeping his covenant of love to a thousand generations of those who love him and keep his commandments" (Deuteronomy 7:9).

The strength of the covenant God made with Israel (and with all who would believe thereafter) doesn't lie in our ability to measure up to God's standard. If it did, we'd all fall hopelessly short. It rests on the unchanging nature of God's character.

Like a loving father, God may discipline us for our unfaithfulness, but He never withdraws His loving-kindness from us. He remains committed to us forever.

When I lose my temper and say and do things that bring shame to His name, God's covenant gives me hope. When I forget all His promises and disintegrate into a blubbering blob of fear, His commitment to love me forever gives me hope. When I choose to satisfy my flesh instead of feeding my spirit, His unwavering presence gives me hope. His marriage covenant with me, based on His unchanging nature, guarantees both my salvation and my sanctification.

Javier didn't deserve Annie's love, but because of the commitment she had made, she extended it anyway. Similarly, we don't deserve God's unfailing love, but because of the covenant He made with believers, He extends it anyway.

Knowing we are united with God forever, we can press on to become all He created us to be—men and women who are fully loved and free to extend that love to others.

Take Heart

God's covenant promise unites us with Him forever. Knowing He'll never leave us gives us hope and security.

From the Heart

Father, you are so faithful. I don't deserve your forever love, but I'm infinitely grateful for it. Knowing you've committed yourself to me forever gives me hope and security when I feel unlovable. Help me live in light of the love you've bestowed on me, and help me model that faithfulness to others. In Jesus's name I pray, amen.

19

God Is On His Throne

**I lift up my eyes to you, to you who sit
enthroned in heaven.**

PSALM 123:1

If I don't get out of the house, I'm going to explode.

My family was squabbling, and I was stuck in the middle. A peace-loving, fix-everything person, I grieved for my stubborn, angry loved ones. My thoughts churned like an overloaded washing machine as I considered one scenario after another. *Should I intervene? Should I remain silent? Should I act? Should I pray?*

What should I do? I texted a friend. *I feel like I have a rubber band strung between my shoulder blades and someone's twisting it—hard.*

I sought refuge in the backyard. Maybe yard work would relieve the stress. *Lord, I need help.*

I grabbed a weeding tool and a pair of clippers. Soon I realized my yard was in as much disarray as my home. Thorny vines wrapped around my hydrangea bushes. Oak tree seedlings sprouted in my flower beds. Virginia creeper engulfed two of my Knock Out rose-bushes. After an hour of pulling, snipping, and digging, my yard looked better, but my heart still ached.

As I walked under the towering oak tree, I brushed against my grandchildren's favorite swing. Unlike the bench swings of my child-hood, this one provides a magic carpet experience. Circular and made of canvas, it hangs suspended from two ropes. If my grandchildren lie side by side on their bellies, three of them can fit on it.

Or one anxious grandma.

I looked to see if any of the neighbors were in their yards. Seeing no one, I laid face up on the swing and pushed off with my foot. It wasn't long before the gentle motion calmed my fretful heart.

My position on the swing forced me to look up instead of around at my weedy yard. A lacy canopy spread above me. Dappled sunlight flickered through the leaves like twinkle lights. A messy ball of a squirrel's nest nestled in the limbs. I watched a male cardinal, bright against the emerald foliage, hop from branch to branch, chirping for his lady friend to follow.

Far beyond the uppermost branches, blue sky dotted with cotton-candy clouds formed a soothing backdrop. Cradled on the swing, I sighed like a fretful child being rocked to sleep.

Nothing about my circumstances changed, but my perspective did. Instead of looking around at the messiness of my world, I looked up—to the God who rules the heavens and the earth and holds me in His hands.

The psalmist who penned Psalm 123 probably didn't have a canvas swing in an oak tree, but he, too, gained a new perspective. "Unto You I lift up my eyes, O You who dwell in the heavens. Behold, as the eyes of servants look to the hand of their masters, as the eyes of a maid to the hand of her mistress, so our eyes look to the Lord our God, until He has mercy on us" (vv. 1–2 NKJV).

There, surrounded by the stillness of the evening and the vastness of the sky, I felt surrounded by God's presence. I knew, regardless of whether peace ruled in my home, His peace could rule in my heart. God was on His throne.

Take Heart

Because God rules supreme over the circumstances of our lives, we can hope in Him.

From the Heart

Father God, I need you. When the world around me spins out of control, I need you. When the people I love are at odds with each other, I need you. When I fear for the future and grieve over the past, I need you. Help me lift my eyes to you and remember that you are Lord over all. Nothing escapes your sight, and nothing is too hard for you. Surround me with peace and grow my trust. Help me rest in your mercy. In the strong name of Jesus I ask, amen.

20

God of
Future Hope

**Know also that wisdom is like honey for
you: If you find it, there is a future hope for
you, and your hope will not be cut off.**

PROVERBS 24:14

Michael Hingson's guide dog, Roselle, was sound asleep under his
desk on the seventy-eighth floor of Tower 1 of the World Trade Center when the first plane hit. Fifteen floors above, chaos erupted, but
on their floor, things were surprisingly calm.

Hingson's first concern was for his staff. Once all were accounted
for, he directed them to follow the emergency evacuation plan they'd
practiced during a safety briefing earlier that month. When the last
staff member left the office, Roselle led Michael to Stairwell B to
begin their 1,463-step descent.[9]

"Roselle was calm as ever and did not sense any danger in the flames, smoke, or anything else around us," Michael said. "I chose to trust her judgment because Roselle and I were a team. I clutched Roselle's harness, and we headed down the stairs."[10]

Emergency lighting did little to illuminate the crowded stairwell, but Michael was no stranger to darkness. Born blind, he'd navigated his world by following a trusted guide. He'd never taken the stairs before, but with Roselle to guide him, he stepped confidently from one stair to the next.

Progress was slow. As the noise of emergency vehicles, groaning steel, and frightened people increased, they often encountered someone overcome with fear and unable to go on.

"Fall in behind us," Michael would say. "Roselle will lead us out. She knows the way." By the time they emerged from the building an hour later, Roselle had led Michael and thirty other people to safety.

Michael had hope because he had Roselle to guide him.

We can have hope because we have God and His wisdom to guide us.

Future hope, the writer of Proverbs tells us, comes from seeking and applying God's wisdom. "Know also that wisdom is like honey for you: If you find it, there is a future hope for you, and your hope will not be cut off" (Proverbs 24:14).

As Michael trusted Roselle to lead him through the darkness of the World Trade Center stairwell, believers can trust God to guide us through the twists, turns, and dark places of life.

When the way seems uncertain, we can seek His insight through the Word, other believers, and the voice of the Holy Spirit. When frightening challenges crash into our lives and we don't know which path to take, God will supply abundant wisdom (James 1:5).

He knows we need His wisdom to steer around the dangers of poor choices and sinful actions. He recognizes we need His insight to navigate cloudy relational challenges, confusing financial situations, and life-threatening health concerns. But He won't force His guidance on us. We must search for it as hidden treasure and apply it to our lives by faith (Proverbs 2:1–5).

Michael trusted Roselle when he couldn't see the way through the darkness of the World Trade Tower. We have a far-wiser guide—a loving Father who abundantly supplies both daily insight and future hope.

Take Heart

God's wisdom guides us through the darkness of today and provides us with a sure and future hope.

From the Heart

Father, sometimes I doubt that your way is best. Instead of going to your Word for wisdom and instruction, I trust my own understanding. I get so blinded by this world that I forget there's a bigger picture. That there's a world beyond this one waiting for me. Open my eyes, Father, to dig into your Word for the wisdom you have for me. Then give me the faith to apply it to my life. For my sake and the sake of those around me I ask these things, amen.

Part 2

God's Work
(What God Does)

21

God Always Hears Our Prayers

**The eyes of the LORD are on the righteous,
and his ears are attentive to their cry.**

PSALM 34:15

My granddaughter Lauren stood before me, wide-eyed and distressed. Her curly hair was everywhere, and a dirt smudge stained her cheek. "I called and called for you, and you didn't come."

I was playing with her three siblings, and the noise from our game had drowned out her cries. "I'm so sorry!" I said, brushing the hair from her face and drawing her into my arms. "I wasn't ignoring you. I just didn't hear you."

Sometimes, when I'm in distress, I wonder if God hears me. When answers to my prayers come slowly, I'm tempted to doubt that He is working on my behalf. Sometimes I neglect our relationship and drift away. Does He hear my prayers then? Even worse, when I choose to sin and intentionally disobey His Word, will He turn a deaf ear when I ask Him to forgive me? Thankfully, the Bible contains example after example of how God hears the cries of His children, no matter where they are.

Elijah, fresh from his victory over the prophets of Baal, fled from wicked Queen Jezebel, who'd threatened to kill him. Exhausted and overwhelmed, he sat down under a broom bush in the wilderness and prayed that he might die. "I have had enough, Lord," he said. "Take my life" (1 Kings 19:4).

God not only heard his prayer from the wilderness, He heard his heart. He sent an angel to provide food and water, invited him to lie down and sleep, and gave him a fresh vision for his ministry.

God heard Hezekiah's prayer from his sick bed. Isaiah the prophet had warned him, "Put your house in order, because you are going to die; you will not recover" (Isaiah 38:1).

"Hezekiah turned his face to the wall and prayed to the Lord, 'Remember, Lord, how I have walked before you faithfully and with wholehearted devotion and have done what is good in your eyes.' And Hezekiah wept bitterly" (vv. 2–3).

"Then the word of the Lord came to Isaiah: 'Go and tell Hezekiah, "This is what the Lord, the God of your father David, says: I have heard your prayer and seen your tears; I will add fifteen years to your life"'" (vv. 4–5). While we know it's not always God's will to heal, we can trust that He hears our sickbed prayers and will answer them according to His will.

God heard the disciples' cry for physical deliverance when the boat they'd been sailing in encountered a fierce storm. As wind and waves from the squall threatened to capsize them, they cried out in distress, "Lord, save us! We're going to drown!" (Matthew 8:25).

Jesus rebuked the wind and the waves, and the sea became completely calm.

God heard Peter's cry for deliverance, too, as he languished in prison, persecuted, arrested for his faith, and awaiting trial. While his Christian brothers and sisters held a late-night vigil, Peter's prayers reached God's ears. God dispatched an angel to execute a heavenly jail break. After the chains that shackled his hands and feet fell off, Peter walked past two sets of guards to where the city gate swung open for him. Only then did his angel escort leave him (Acts 12:1–10).

Perhaps the most profound example of God's ability and willingness to hear the prayers of His children regardless of where they pray took place deep beneath the sea. Jonah, the prodigal prophet running from God's call to preach to the wicked Ninevites, expressed his repentant prayer from inside the belly of a great fish.

With seaweed wrapped around his head and swimming in gastric juices, he cried out, "In my distress I called to the Lord, and he answered me. From deep in the realm of the dead I called for help, and you listened to my cry" (Jonah 2:2).

God forgave Jonah for his rebellion and repeated his call to ministry. Demonstrating that He is a God of second chances, He commanded the fish to burp Jonah out onto the shore, where Jonah fulfilled his calling to preach to the Ninevites. Jonah's testimony is a dramatic declaration that God always hears the prayers of His children when we repent, no matter where our sin has taken us.

In His mercy, God even hears the prayers of the lost when they cry to Him from the depths of their sinfulness. Condemned to die for a crime he'd committed, the thief hanging on the cross beside Jesus knew he was a sinner. "We are punished justly, for we are getting what our deeds deserve," he said to the second thief.

Then he acknowledged his sin, repented, and prayed to Jesus in faith. "Jesus, remember me when you come into your kingdom" (Luke 23:42).

"Truly I tell you," Jesus responded, "today you will be with me in paradise."

Stories like these and hundreds more give me solid hope that God will hear my prayers regardless of where I am when I pray. The noise of activity prevented me from hearing my granddaughter Lauren call out to me for help, but nothing keeps God from hearing our cries.

"Where can I go from your Spirit?" the psalmist testified. "Where can I flee from your presence? If I go up to the heavens, you are there; if I make my bed in the depths, you are there. If I rise on the wings of the dawn, if I settle on the far side of the sea, even there your hand will guide me, your right hand will hold me fast" (Psalm 139:7–10).

Take Heart

Whether we pray from the depths of a sickbed, a jail cell, or a watery grave, He not only hears us, He responds in ways that will fulfill His good purpose for our lives.

From the Heart

Father, when circumstances make me feel like you're out of earshot of my prayers, remind me that you always hear me. Your ears are attentive to my cries, and your heart is eager to respond to my requests. When Satan whispers that I've failed you one too many times to expect you to hear my prayers, remind me of Psalm 34:15. Thank you for the hope this promise brings me. Help me pray in light of this truth.

22

While We Were Still Sinners . . .

**But God demonstrates his own
love for us in this: While we were still
sinners, Christ died for us.**

ROMANS 5:8

I was doomed.

My childhood church taught me that if my good works outweighed my bad, I'd go to heaven when I died. So I obeyed my parents (for the most part), did well in school, and didn't fight with my sisters (much). But I was also selfish, self-centered, self-righteous, and self-absorbed. (Do you see a pattern here?) I willingly received and grudgingly gave. I argued for fifteen minutes about doing a chore that took five minutes to do.

My good works couldn't keep up with my bad. I was condemned.

As I entered my teenage years, life continued to revolve around me and what made me happy. What advanced my agenda. What best positioned me for a life of happiness, prosperity, and peace.

Except I had none. Peace, that is. Despite having everything that promised to fulfill me, I felt miserable.

My Kingdom of One was about to come crashing down—and that was a good thing. A really good thing.

My boyfriend invited me to his church, so I went. It was quite different than mine, but I didn't care. I'd go wherever he went. Not because I had any spiritual interest, but because of other interests.

Week after week the pastor preached, and I feigned interest. But the longer I attended, the more the pastor's words sunk in, and the truth of the gospel pricked my heart. God's Word never returns empty. It always achieves the purpose for which God sent it (Isaiah 55:11).

"For all have sinned and fall short of the glory of God," the pastor said one evening (Romans 3:23).

No doubt about that. I knew I sinned. Often.

"There is no one righteous, not even one" (Romans 3:10).

None? Not even the sweet-faced church ladies who shared my pew?

"If we say that we have no sin, we deceive ourselves, and the truth is not in us" (1 John 1:8 NKJV).

Okay already, I get the point.

"For whoever keeps the whole law and yet stumbles at just one point is guilty of breaking all of it" (James 2:10).

Just one point? Are you kidding? No one can meet that standard.

"People are destined to die once, and after that to face judgment" (Hebrews 9:27).

Gulp.

One day, as I talked with my pastor, a thousand pinpricks of the Word of God culminated in a great heart hemorrhage. For the first time, I saw my sins for what they were. The illusion of being able to do more good than bad to earn God's favor crumbled in the face of impossibility.

In the heap of hopeless rubble, I found grace and love from a holy God. From the same God who had given me life and would one day demand an accounting for how I had spent that life. The one I'd insulted by my many sins, which I'd labeled "personal choice" and "freedom to make my own decisions."

In a God-sent moment of spiritual clarity, I realized that every kindness that had entered my world, including God's offer of salvation, were gifts. God had given me every breath, every heartbeat, and every moment of success out of an abundance of love and mercy, not because I'd earned it through my good works.

"But God demonstrates his own love for us in this:" Romans 5:8 declares, "But God demonstrates his own love for us in this: *While we were still sinners*, Christ died for us" (emphasis added).

I saw for the first time I didn't have to do good works to earn God's love. I couldn't—that's why Jesus had to die. He offered us His perfect life as a ransom for our wretched one. All I had to do was repent of my sins and accept what He had already done.

I've never felt so hopeless and so hopeful as the day I realized I was powerless to work my way out of spiritual poverty. I was finally ready to receive God's lavish gift of salvation. My good works had gotten me nowhere. But faith in Christ's perfect work did.

Right there in the pastor's office, my life changed. I was no longer doomed. I had hope not only for my physical future, but for my eternal future. I was saved.

Take Heart

We don't have to clean up our life so God will love us. He loved us enough to die for us while we were still sinners. This gives us hope for a forever life with Him.

From the Heart

Thank you, Father, for your incomprehensible love. Common sense says, "Clean up your act so God will love you," but your Word says, "You can't clean up your act, but I love you anyway." The lyrics to a hymn rise in my heart, "Amazing love! How can it be? That thou, my God, should die for me." Thank you for the hope that comes from receiving your unmerited favor. May my life reflect that love to others. Help me love and serve you— out of gratitude, not fear—all the days of my life. In the precious name of Jesus I ask, amen.

23

God Will Complete His Work

**Being confident of this, that he who began
a good work in you will carry it on to
completion until the day of Christ Jesus.**

PHILIPPIANS 1:6

Kaylee Johnston jumped as if I'd snuck up behind her and yelled, "Boo."

I most certainly hadn't. But when I stood in the doorway of the dental office waiting room and called her name, she jumped from the chair, startling me and the other patients. She acted as nervous as any first-time dental patient I'd ever seen.

When she opened her mouth, I understood why.

"I'm a single mom, and money's been tight," she said as I seated her in my dental chair. "I kinda let myself go." She stared at her hands clenched tightly in her lap.

"I just started a new job with the state, and I have dental insurance now." She lifted her gaze to meet mine, and a hopeful light glinted in her eyes. "It's time I did something for myself. I want to fix my teeth."

As I x-rayed, examined, and cleaned her teeth, I kept the conversation light and positive, but inside, my heart was sinking. *There's so much wrong with this poor woman's mouth,* I thought. *Lord, help me tell her what she needs to know without discouraging her.* I took a deep breath.

"Kaylee, I'm so excited you came to our office. That took a lot of courage. You have quite a few teeth that need repair. We can't do it overnight, but in time, we can make your mouth healthy and beautiful again. It'll take patience and dedication, but it'll be worth it."

For the first time that morning, Kaylee smiled—a shy smile, just a lift of the corners of her mouth—but a hopeful one.

Little by little my boss filled, restored, and replaced her decayed teeth. One infected tooth required a root canal and a crown. Another badly damaged tooth had to be extracted. He saved the costliest treatments for last, giving her time to budget and save. Three years and one month from the day she walked into our office, her transformation was complete.

"You don't need to come back for six months," I announced. "All you need now is preventive maintenance."

I smiled widely as I delivered the news, but not as wide as Kaylee. Her smile stretched from ear to ear, showing off every one of her healthy, beautiful teeth.

Before I placed my faith in Christ, I had bigger problems than a mouthful of decayed teeth. I had holes in my character, disposition, and nature. I was selfish and opinionated. My temper was short, and my patience level even shorter. I was lazy, anxious, and self-absorbed. And that was just the short list.

The future frightened and overwhelmed me. I knew I had no foundation on which to build my life.

One day I'd had enough. As my pastor led me in a prayer, I repented of my sin and surrendered my life to Christ.

"God, for years I've been living my life my way, and I've made a mess of it. I don't want to be in control anymore," I prayed. "Forgive me of my sins and make me a new person."

When I placed my faith in Christ, the Holy Spirit came to live inside me and began the restoration process. Almost immediately, my life began to change. Little by little, He cleaned out the spiritual decay of bad habits, closet sins, and ungodly attitudes.

I broke off a relationship I knew didn't please God. I desired to read the Bible and attend church. I stopped watching movies and listening to music that dishonored God.

Although I continued to struggle with selfishness, anger, and worry, when I gave in to these sins, I experienced the gentle conviction of the Holy Spirit. Like a kind father who wants the best for his child, God made me aware of my sin, enabled me to confess and turn away from it, and extended His forgiveness. He extracted the poisonous roots of sinful behavior and replaced them with acts of love and godliness.

Transformation (the Bible calls it *sanctification*) doesn't happen overnight (or even over decades). It takes a lifetime.

When we grow discouraged by our ongoing battles with sin, Philippians 1:6 gives us hope. "Being confident of this," the apostle Paul wrote to fellow believers, "that he who began a good work in you *will carry it on to completion* until the day of Christ Jesus" (emphasis added).

As we immerse ourselves in God's Word, obey what He calls us to do, and repent when we fail, God continues the good work He's doing in our lives.

One day, when He calls all believers home to live with Him forever, we'll stand before Him sinless and complete. And if you're anything like me, you'll smile—a great big, ear-to-ear smile—that will testify to the great work He has done in your life.

Take Heart

God will not leave me to my own powerless efforts of self-improvement. Instead, through the Holy Spirit who lives inside me, He will complete the good work He began in me at my salvation.

From the Heart

Thank you, Lord, for promising to finish the good work you began in me at my salvation. Sometimes I get so frustrated and discouraged with myself. I make progress, then I slip back into old habits and negative behavior patterns. Like a patient father, you remain by my side, sanding and polishing my character until it looks more like you than like me. I can't wait for the day when I will be complete. Thank you for never giving up on me. I love you so much.

24

The Gift
of His Spirit

**What we have received is not the
spirit of the world, but the Spirit who is
from God, so that we may understand
what God has freely given us.**

1 CORINTHIANS 2:12

"Hi, Mandy," I said into the phone. "How's Winston?" Our family was vacationing out of state, and my kind friend was dog sitting our freckle-faced spaniel-setter.

"Well, he's not real happy with me right now," she said, "and to be honest, I'm not real happy with him either. As soon as I let him out the door this morning, he made a beeline for a pile of chicken poop and rolled in it. I've bathed him twice, and I still can't get the stink out."

I was glad he hadn't made a beeline for one of her pet chickens, but why, oh why, would my sweet, intelligent dog deliberately roll in something so disgusting? If I had the spirit of a dog, I'm sure I could come up with a dozen reasons, but since I have the spirit of a human being, all I can say is, "Gross."

Hunting is another thing I don't understand. Male friends of mine invest thousands of dollars in hunting equipment. Some pay exorbitant fees to join clubs to hunt deer and birds. A friend spent his inheritance to buy acreage to develop into hunting land.

All year long he plants and harvests crops to entice deer, turkey, and ducks to visit his property. When hunting season comes, he dons camouflage clothing, sprays himself to mask his scent, and heads out before dawn to sit in a tree for hours hoping a deer will walk by.

Deer season begins on August 15 in my home state of South Carolina. The average temperature is four degrees shy of one hundred. Mosquitoes and ticks lurk everywhere. Duck season begins in late November. The perfect time to hunt ducks, they tell me, is on cold, rainy days. Sometimes hunters must wade into freezing cold water to retrieve their birds.

By now my male readers are nodding enthusiastically, and my female readers (including me) are scratching our heads. We females (with a nod to the rare woman who enjoys hunting) simply don't get it. We don't understand their passion because we don't have the spirit of a man.

After I became a Christian, several of my friends felt a similar confusion about my passion for spiritual things.

"Why do you go to church *three times a week*, for crying out loud?" one asked.

"You always have your nose buried in your Bible," another observed. "I don't get it. I've tried to read it and gotten nothing out of it. All those *begats* and *begots*."

I remember feeling the same way. Before surrendering my life to Christ, I tried to read the Bible several times, but never made it past Genesis. I highlighted a few clever turns of phrase in the poetry books. "There is a time for everything, and a season for every activity under the heavens" (wasn't that a sixties song?), "Love your neighbor as yourself," and "Do to others what you would have them do to you," but the message and majesty of the Bible were lost on me. Within myself, I had no hope of understanding it.

Then I came to Christ. I discovered the Bible is a living book, filled with truth, power, and passion. I found wisdom sprinkled on every page. I found answers to questions like, "Why is there evil in the world?" "Where do we go when we die?" and "How can I find true joy?" As I read and studied, God unlocked mysteries of His Word that had been hidden to me as an unbeliever. I didn't miraculously understand everything; I never will. But something had changed.

What made the difference? Why had my understanding opened when before it had been sealed shut?

I had God's Spirit. Paul's first letter to the Corinthian church explains it this way: "What we have received is not the spirit of the world, but the Spirit who is from God, so that we may understand what God has freely given us" (1:12). God has given us His Word to guide and enlighten us, and He's given us His Spirit to be our teacher. "This is what we speak," Paul said, "not in words taught us by human wisdom but in words taught by the Spirit, explaining spiritual realities with Spirit-taught words" (v. 13).

And what about the unsaved who don't have the Spirit living inside them? "The person without the Spirit does not accept the things that come from the Spirit of God but considers them foolishness, and cannot understand them because they are discerned only through the Spirit," Paul explained to the fledgling church (v. 14).

"But we have the mind of Christ" (v. 16). When we accept Christ as Savior, the Holy Spirit comes to live within us, giving us supernatural insight into spiritual things. Although we still must "do [our] best to present [ourselves] to God as one approved, a worker who does not need to be ashamed and who correctly handles the word of truth" (2 Timothy 2:15), believers have been given insight into the mind of the Lord. God himself gives us insight into truth.

When we struggle to make sense of challenging passages or difficult doctrines, we can pray to the Holy Spirit, our teacher, and ask Him to make the passage clear to us. We can meditate on Scripture, read what other godly teachers have written, and dig deeply into biblical resources. God promises to enlighten our minds and lead us into all truth.

"The Advocate, the Holy Spirit, whom the Father will send in my name, will teach you all things and will remind you of everything I have said to you," Jesus promised His disciples in John 14:26.

I'll be the first to admit that I don't understand everything. Because I don't have the spirit of a dog or the spirit of a man, I have no hope of understanding why a dog rolls in chicken poop or a man who lives within two miles of a grocery store tromps around in the woods all day hunting deer. But because I have the Spirit of God living inside me, I can hope to understand many of the supernatural mysteries of God.

Imagine that.

Take Heart

We can understand the truth of God's Word through the Holy Spirit who lives inside us.

From the Heart

Thank you, God, for giving me the Holy Spirit to be my teacher. Every time I struggle to understand your Word or your ways, I can ask the Spirit for help, and He's already there. Because of Him, I can hope to understand spiritual truths with my human mind. I love you so much, amen.

25

In the Waiting Times

**But when the fullness of time had
come, God sent forth his Son, born of
woman, born under the law, to redeem
those who were under the law, so that
we might receive adoption as sons.**

GALATIANS 4:4-5 ESV

Do you remember how long it took for Christmas to come when you
were a child?

From Thanksgiving Day on, the excitement would build. Decorations appeared in stores. Then lights popped up around town, draped
in trees like fairy necklaces. Mouthwatering smells wafted out of
neighbors' kitchens. Christmas trees strapped to station-wagon roofs
rolled by like a parade.

At our house, Dad would finally drag the family tree out of the
attic and set it up in the living room. One by one (or sometimes in

clumps) packages would appear under the Christmas tree. Stockings dangled from the mantle like limp balloons waiting for the breath of Christmas to fill them.

It was a horribly marvelous wait, those childhood seasons of Advent.

And although my childhood Advents were glitterier than the wait the children of Israel experienced, the delays were holy pauses nonetheless.

My sisters and I hoped for a bicycle, the latest Barbie doll, or a stocking full of candy, but the children of Israel waited for the greatest gift of all—the Messiah.

And for humanity, it had been a very long wait. From the dawn of creation, really.

"And I will put enmity between you and the woman, and between your offspring and hers; he will crush your head, and you will strike his heel," God had promised in Genesis 3:15.

The time between this first messianic promise and its fulfillment stretched for centuries. Years of glory and years of shame. Times of glorious triumph and times of gut-wrenching tragedy. Moments of fearless faith and moments of faithless fear.

And then the silence. Four hundred years with no word from God. No kingly edict. No prophetic visions. No holy mandates.

Just silence.

And waiting. And waiting. And waiting.

Unlike my childhood wait between one Christmas and the next, where the memory of the past season birthed hope and expectation for the next, the Jewish people had no memories of their own to carry them through. All they had were their forebearers' stories and the ancient promises that, one day, a Messiah would come.

"For to us a child is born, to us a son is given, and the government will be on his shoulders. And he will be called Wonderful Counselor, Mighty God, Everlasting Father, Prince of Peace. Of the greatness of his government and peace there will be no end" (Isaiah 9:6–7).

Yet during that long silence, and the even longer wait between mankind's fall and Jesus's incarnation, God was at work. Preparing a place. Preparing a people. Even preparing a Roman infrastructure that enabled early believers to carry the news of the gospel to the far corners of the globe.

And then, in the fullness of time, God sent His Son to save the world. "But when the fullness of time had come, God sent forth his Son, born of woman, born under the law, to redeem those who were under the law, so that we might receive adoption as sons" (Galatians 4:4–5 ESV).

In the fullness of time.

I don't know what you're waiting for right now. A prodigal child to return? A dream to be fulfilled? A marriage to be healed? A loved one to be saved? A relationship to be restored? A financial burden to be lifted?

Whatever it is, don't assume God's silence means he's not working. Cling to faith, for "without faith it is impossible to please God, because anyone who comes to him must believe that he exists and that he rewards those who earnestly seek him," the writer of Hebrews reminds us (11:6).

You may be in the middle of a long silence, a time when you wonder if God is at work. Don't stop praying. Continue to search God's Word for promises and claim them. Enlist prayer warriors to battle with you.

Never lose hope. Trust that, despite what you see, God is at work. Believe that, in the fullness of time, God will speak life into the silence that fills your ears. Don't believe Satan's lies that God has forgotten you or that He's uncaring or impotent. Trust that He's always at work (John 5:17) and will fulfill His plan for your life. No plan of God's can be thwarted (Job 42:2).

He'll bring to fruition what He promised. And when He does, it will be glorious.

Wait. Hope. Trust. God never wastes a season of waiting.

Take Heart

We can remain hopeful because God is at work in the waiting.

From the Heart

Father, thank you for reminding me that even in the waiting times, you are working. Help me trust you, even when I don't see evidence of your hand at work. Remind me that you are with me. Teach me the lessons I need to learn to accomplish all you have for me to do. Grow my faith and trust today as I hope in you. In the strong name of Jesus I ask, amen.

26

God Commands
Dry Bones to Live

**He asked me, "Son of man,
can these bones live?"**

EZEKIEL 37:3

"Son of man, can these bones live?"

To Ezekiel, surrounded by a valley of dry bones, God's question seemed . . . absurd. Heart-wrenching and hopeless. Maybe even cruel.

I've stood at the bedsides and caskets of dead loved ones. If anyone had asked me, "Can these bones live?" I would have answered, as Martha did long ago, "I know he will rise again in the resurrection at the last day" (John 11:24). But not now. He's dead.

Ezekiel wasn't sitting beside a deceased loved one or standing by the coffin of someone who had passed away. He was surrounded by a vast expanse of beyond-dead bones—bones that had laid there so long they were one footfall away from dust.

And yet God asked, "Can these bones live?"

Ezekiel, faith-filled prophet and priest that he was, answered God's question in a way that defied the obvious and left room for a miracle.

"Sovereign LORD, you alone know" (Ezekiel 37:3).

How many times have you looked at a loved one or a friend and seen what Ezekiel saw—a valley of dry bones? Not physical bones like those that littered the plains of Ezekiel's vision, but spiritual ones. Dry bones that housed a soul running hard away from God and in danger of disintegrating when the next crisis came.

How often have you cried over, prayed for, begged, and witnessed to someone you love who seemed determined to march straight into eternity separated from God? How many times have you stopped praying, thinking there was no hope, only to shoulder the prayer burden again, clinging to the knowledge that God calls us to pray for the lost?

With rare exception, physical resurrection belongs to the realm of the miraculous, but spiritual resurrections, while also miraculous, happen all the time.

The apostle Paul was one whom Christ resurrected. His spiritual bones, though zealous and religious, were deader than dead. "For you have heard of my previous way of life in Judaism, how intensely I persecuted the church of God and tried to destroy it" (Galatians 1:13).

Yet the God whose followers Paul persecuted called his name. God rebuked him for his sin, filled him with faith, and breathed spiritual life into his soul. Paul passed from death to life in a transformation so glorious he never stopped talking about it.

Unlike Paul, I had no religion to cover my spiritually dry bones. I was lost without pretense or hope. I couldn't claim, as he did, that

I was seeking to please God. I was seeking to please myself. I was number one, and there was no number two.

Yet, to borrow from Paul's testimony in Galatians 1:15, God, "set me apart from my mother's womb and called me by his grace." Before I was even born, God had a plan for my life, and it involved loving and serving Him.

God's been breathing life into dry bones for millennia. He began with Adam in the garden. He plucked Abraham out of the pagan land of the Chaldees and made him His friend. He called Methuselah, an aged man of centuries, David from the sheepfolds, and Ruth, a widow and an outsider, and made them compatriots in the vast army of believers.

He's summoned into life the dry bones of princesses and prostitutes, drug addicts and doctors. No heart is too hard, and no sin too great for God's breath to resurrect. Again and again, I've seen Him replace hearts of stone with hearts of flesh (Ezekiel 11:19; 36:26), transforming haters of God into lovers of God.

If someone you care about looks like a pile of spiritually dry bones, and you wonder if they could ever live, I invite you to stand in the valley with Ezekiel. Lift your eyes from the dead bones to the living Savior and say in faith and hope, "Sovereign Lord, you alone know."

> So I prophesied as I was commanded. And as I was prophesying, there was a noise, a rattling sound, and the bones came together, bone to bone. I looked, and tendons and flesh appeared on them and skin covered them, but there was no breath in them.
>
> Then he said to me, "Prophesy to the breath; prophesy, son of man, and say to it, 'This is what the Sovereign LORD says:

Come, breath, from the four winds and breathe into these
slain, that they may live.'" So I prophesied as he commanded
me, and breath entered them; they came to life and stood up
on their feet—a vast army. (Ezekiel 37:7–10)

Unlike Ezekiel, we can't command spiritual life into anyone, but
God can. He resurrected the spiritual bones of the Israelites, and He
can do it for our loved ones as well.

Will you join me, in faith, trust, and hope and ask the Lord God
to breathe life into our loved ones' souls? He has the power to cause
dry bones to come alive.

Take Heart

We can have hope for our loved ones' spiritually dead souls because
we pray to a God who commands dry bones to live.

From the Heart

*Father, I confess that sometimes I pray to you as if I'm praying to someone
who is powerless and weak. Help me remember that raising to life a field of
dry bones is just one small accomplishment in your mighty list of miracles.
Nothing is too hard for you. In Jesus, you called yourself the Resurrection
and the Life. Breathe life into my loved ones' souls. Resurrect their spirits,
I pray. Make their dry bones live! Amen.*

27

God
Graciously Waits

**Therefore the LORD will wait, that He may
be gracious to you.**

ISAIAH 30:18 NKJV

The neighbors must have thought my mother was carving me up and feeding me to the penguins. Passionate cries emanated from my bedroom. My chest heaved in anguish, forcing out sounds I didn't know I could make. Tears streamed from my eyes, mingling with the snot that poured from my nose, turning my face into a salty, gooey mess. I alternated between burying my slimy face in my pillow and pointing it to the sky in lament.

The world was coming to an end, and it was all my mother's fault.

Well, not really. But it seemed that way to my ten-year-old soul.

I don't remember the transgression that prompted my normally easygoing mother to come down hard on me that day, but I'm sure

I deserved it. As she meted out my punishment, she said words that took my breath away.

"No television for you tonight."

"But today's Friday," I said. "We always watch television on Friday. It's the best night of the week. My favorite shows are on. I can't miss them!"

My breath came in panicked gasps, and my voice rose as I realized the magnitude of my punishment.

"Pleeeeeeeeeeeeeeease don't make me miss my favorite shows," I wailed.

But to no avail. My mother walked from the room, leaving me to wallow in my very vocal misery.

An hour or so later I came to her, spent and broken. "I'm sorry," I whimpered. "I won't do it again."

She smoothed the hair from my flushed face and drew me into a hug. "I know," she said.

When my family gathered around the nineteen-inch black-and-white television that evening, I sat in their midst, humbled and grateful for my mother's mercy.

The time between my sin and my repentance was miserable, but it was necessary. Although at the time I thought my mother was cruel, I recognize now she was anything but. While I fussed and fumed, she waited patiently, allowing the weight of her just punishment to do its work.

Like the Lord, she knew that experiencing the consequences of my sin might bring me to repentance. And after repentance could come restoration.

And so she waited.

Today's Scripture tells us the Lord waited while the children of Israel went their rebellious ways. But He didn't wait vengefully, sharpening his lightning bolts, anxious to pour out his wrath and judgment. He waited patiently, eager for an opportunity to be gracious to them.

All it took to open the spillway of grace were two deeply felt, totally sincere words: "I'm sorry."

I marvel at the supernatural beauty of God's heart. While his justice requires Him to punish our sin, His mercy looks for every opportunity to show grace when we sincerely repent. Because Christ took our ultimate punishment on the cross, God the Father is free to slather mercy on every humble soul who comes to Him in sincerity and faith.

"In returning and rest you shall be saved," He promises. "In quietness and confidence shall be your strength" (Isaiah 30:15 NKJV).

Take Heart

God waits for opportunities to be gracious to us.

From the Heart

Thank you, Father, for your patience with me. I deserve your judgment, yet you look for every opportunity to pour out your mercy on me instead. Thank you for sending Jesus to take my punishment, satisfy your righteous requirement of justice, and make a way for grace.

28

He Remembers
Our Sin No More

**I, even I, am he who blots out your
transgressions, for my own sake, and
remembers your sins no more.**

ISAIAH 43:25

I was a model dental hygiene student—until Tooth Morphology class. I didn't mind memorizing the components of teeth or their dimensions. Remembering that the cusp of Carabelli was usually found on the maxillary first molars wasn't a problem either. But carving teeth out of soap? Just shoot me now.

Thankfully, the third-semester class was almost over. Our final project, designed to prove we understood basic tooth anatomy, required us to carve an incisor, a premolar, and a molar—to scale—out of a bar of Ivory soap.

I've never been a fan of long projects with tedious details. I'd rather clean ten toilets than sew one hem. And those million-piece puzzles other people put together for fun? No, thank you. More than any other assignment, the tooth carving project taxed my patience to the limits. I knew if I shaved off a millimeter too much from any surface, I'd have to start all over again. The pressure of perfection soured my disposition.

Ultimately, the intricately shaped premolar became my undoing.

"This is a total waste of time," I said to my classmates seated at the table with me. "Why should I spend five hours of my life carving soap when I could be in the clinic learning a skill I'll actually use one day?"

"Lori."

I froze at the sound of my instructor's voice behind me.

"Come with me into my office."

Dr. H., the program director, was small of stature, but large in presence.

I rose and followed him down the hall like a condemned prisoner. He pointed to a seat facing his desk. I sat, eyes focused on my tightly clenched hands, and waited for the reprimand I deserved.

"You have the worst attitude of any student in this program," he said. "You've been grumbling about this project for a week, and I've had enough. I won't let your muttering affect the rest of the students. Frankly, I doubt you have what it takes to graduate, and I'll be surprised if you make it through. Would you like to quit now and make it easier on all of us?"

"No, Sir," I said. "I'll do better. I promise."

I slunk from the room when he dismissed me.

From then on, every time I encountered Dr. H., I felt his eyes on me. Measuring me. Remembering my bad attitude. Waiting for me to mess up again so he could boot me out of the program.

In life, my transgressions have been much more serious than youthful grumbling and a sour attitude. Compared to God's perfect standard, I fall short every day. Every hour, probably.

In the eighteen years before I knew Christ as my Savior, I committed some whopping sins. After I surrendered my life to Christ, even though He's been transforming me, I still sin. Anger, impatience, faithlessness, worry, envy, and spiritual laziness follow me like kids trailing an ice cream truck.

Sometimes, when I measure who I am compared to who God created me to be, I feel discouraged. Even hopeless.

But Isaiah 43:25 restores my hope: "I, even I, am he who blots out your transgressions, for my own sake," God declared, "and remembers your sins no more."

Remembers your sins no more.

Psalm 103:12 describes how He does it: "As far as the east is from the west, so far has he removed our transgressions from us," the psalmist declared.

Do you know how far the east is from the west? You're right—they never meet.

This is how far God has removed our sins from us—the distance of infinity. When we confess and turn away from our sins, God sends them off into the outer reaches of space and forgets them.

And if this life-changing, guilt-crushing, hope-inspiring fact isn't enough, the psalmist shows us God's heart: "As a father has compassion on his children, so the LORD has compassion on those who fear him; for he knows how we are formed, he remembers that we are dust" (vv. 13–14).

God knows we're frail. That we struggle every day to live a Spirit-filled, God-controlled life. He understands, as Paul so eloquently confessed, that we have the desire to do what is good but often fail to carry it out. That we don't do the good things we want to do but often practice the sin we don't want to practice (Romans 7:18–19).

He never excuses our sin, but as we battle it in the transforming power of the Holy Spirit, He forgives and forgets it.

I don't know if Dr. H. ever forgot my infractions. For the duration of my time in the program, did he remember me as *the one with the bad attitude?*

I'm grateful God, because Christ paid the penalty for my sins, chooses to forget them. All of them. For the duration of my time on Earth, He remembers me as *the one whose sins I've forgotten.*

Take Heart

Although others may remember my sins, God, because of Christ, forgives and forgets them all.

From the Heart

Father, sometimes I struggle to forget the sins of my past. Memories and regrets threaten to drown me in remorse. When I feel this way, remind me that I'm not that person anymore. I'm a new creation. You've canceled my sin debt and chosen to forget my sin. While I may never forget what I've done, help me see my sin—past, present, and future—the way you see it: paid for by the blood of Jesus. And when I do sin, help me confess it quickly and walk in victory. Thank you for the hope I feel, knowing that when you look at me, you see me sinless and pure. Because of Jesus I pray, amen.

He Renews Us Day by Day

Therefore we do not lose heart. Though outwardly we are wasting away, yet inwardly we are being renewed day by day.

2 CORINTHIANS 4:16

Everyone in our small church wanted to sit by Steve Bradley when they worshipped. Not because he had the finest singing voice around, although his midrange baritone was certainly acceptable. We liked sitting near him because he sang passionately, joyfully, and *loudly*.

Those of us with less-than-perfect voices could sing as loud as we wanted if we sat beside Steve. We had no fear someone would hear us sing off-key. His worship covered our shortcomings. One day, in appreciation and love, we presented him with a T-shirt that said, *Real Men Sing Loud*.

Thirty years have passed since those glorious days, but Steve's still singing. Not as loudly, because a stroke has weakened one side of his body. A damaged valve in his heart awaits replacement, and age has stolen his youthful vigor. A bout with COVID set him back, and the aches and pains of his eighty-something-year-old body make it harder to raise his hands in praise. Although his outer man is wasting away, his inner man grows stronger every day.

Steve embodies what the apostle Paul wrote about in 2 Corinthians 4:16: "Therefore we do not lose heart. Though outwardly we are wasting away, yet inwardly we are being renewed day by day."

I suspect if Paul and Steve sat down together over a cup of coffee, they'd find a lot to talk about. One topic might be the challenges of living in a deteriorating body. Paul, too, felt the frustration of wanting to do more, yet being "limited" by his physical frailties.

Paul wasn't eighty years old when he penned his letters to the Corinthians, but he was already experiencing the effects of his labor for Christ. Listen to his testimony:

> I have worked much harder, been in prison more frequently, been flogged more severely, and been exposed to death again and again. Five times I received from the Jews the forty lashes minus one. Three times I was beaten with rods, once I was pelted with stones, three times I was shipwrecked, I spent a night and a day in the open sea, I have been constantly on the move. (2 Corinthians 11:23–26)

In verses 27 through 29, we read more about Paul's physical deprivations: "I have labored and toiled and have often gone without sleep; I have known hunger and thirst and have often gone without food; I have been cold and naked. Besides everything else, I face daily the pressure of my concern for all the churches. Who is weak, and I do not feel weak?"

Paul's faithful service to God's kingdom had taken a significant toll on his physical body.

Yet, Paul declared, and Steve's actions do, too, we press on, knowing that as our bodies grow weaker, our spirits grow stronger.

Despite his physical challenges, Paul continued to faithfully serve God, and so does Steve. He teaches Bible studies, often leaning on his cane or the lectern for support. He meets with couples for marriage and family counseling. He mentors the young (and not-so-young) men in his church. He corresponds by email with many of his past Bible college students, former church members, and family.

And he prays. Oh, how he prays. He asks God to raise up a generation of Christians who will proclaim the Word of God fearlessly. He begs God to draw his loved ones into deep and rich relationships with himself. He intercedes for his church, his country, and the world.

The closer Steve draws to death, the more alive he becomes. The years he's invested in the study and practice of God's Word bear increasing fruit both in his heart and in the hearts of those he's influenced. As the veil between this life and the next grows thin, God's face becomes more and more clear. He longs for heaven, yet he knows God still has work for him to do here.

Outwardly he is a frail, elderly man. Inwardly he is a mighty warrior. "We have this treasure in jars of clay," Paul wrote, and Steve would agree, "to show that this all-surpassing power is from God and not from us" (2 Corinthians 4:7).

If we pursue God earnestly every day, we, too, can experience what Paul testified of and Steve lives. Our souls will grow stronger even as our bodies weaken. As I ponder my own mortality, this truth gives me hope. God can and will accomplish His work in my life no matter how old and decrepit I become.

As the apostle Paul did, my friend Steve spends himself for the gospel's sake. He has determined to serve the Lord faithfully as long as he has life and breath in his body. Because he has, his spirit grows stronger every day, and his life testifies to the glory and grace of our Lord Jesus Christ. One day we'll stand before God in heaven and sing praises to His name. I hope I get to stand next to Steve.

Take Heart

Although our physical bodies will grow frail, our souls will grow ever stronger.

From the Heart

Father, each year I grow increasingly more aware that my body is aging. I can't do everything I used to do (at least not without pain). I grow tired more easily. I can't stay up half the night without feeling the effects the next day. Thank you for the hope that even as my body weakens, my soul will continue to grow stronger. Thank you for the work you are doing in and through me every day. In Jesus's name I pray, amen.

30

God Welcomes Prodigals

**He lifted me out of the slimy pit, out of the mud
and mire; he set my feet on a rock and gave me
a firm place to stand. He put a new song in my
mouth, a hymn of praise to our God. Many will
see and fear the Lord and put their trust in him.**

PSALM 40:2-3

Janna was so lost.

Not in a physical sense, although her parents often wondered where she was when she didn't come home. She was lost in a spiritual sense.

Her parents, Rob and Lisa, had raised her in the Lord, but something shifted around age sixteen.

"I don't fit in with that crowd," she'd say when they encouraged her to go to youth group. "All they care about is hair and makeup, and I'm not into that. Besides," she paused, raising her eyes for a second and then looking away, "they're mean."

No amount of pleading would change her mind. "I don't need them," she said. "I'm fine on my own."

Before long, her grades began to slip. She spent more time alone or with Alvonia, a friend from school. When her parents commented on Alvonia's appearance, Janna defended her.

"She's not shallow like the girls at church. She cares about other things."

"Other things" apparently didn't include attending school and getting good grades. The day Janna's teacher called to see when Janna would return after her "illness," Lisa realized her daughter had been skipping school. Although Janna had left the house every day at 7:30, she never made it to class. She'd been hanging out at Alvonia's house instead—with Alvonia's older brother and his dropout friends.

Then they found the drug paraphernalia in her room.

Five years later, Janna was still lost. While her parents consulted counselor after counselor, swinging from forgiveness to tough love, she continued to spiral downward. Alcohol, drugs, and men whose names she couldn't remember changed her from a bubbly, auburn-haired beauty to an empty shell.

But that all changed the morning of May 16.

Sunlight beamed into the dingy apartment, piercing Janna's hungover brain like a dagger. She groaned and rolled over. Forcing her eyes open, she squinted at the movie poster thumbtacked to the wall. It took a moment for her vision to clear enough to see it—a woman swimming frantically on the surface of the water while a giant shark, mouth agape and teeth glinting, prepared to devour her.

Turning her head, she scanned the room. Liquor bottles lay scattered on the floor. Pills littered the coffee table like Skittles at a five-year-old's birthday party. On the sofa, someone she didn't recognize snored.

She glanced back at the poster, and tears clouded her vision. Her stomach churned. Words from the Bible she'd heard in Sunday school long ago cut through the fog of her aching head.

> When he came to his senses, he said, "How many of my
> father's hired servants have food to spare, and here I am starv-
> ing to death! I will set out and go back to my father and say to
> him: Father, I have sinned against heaven and against you. I
> am no longer worthy to be called your son; make me like one
> of your hired servants." (Luke 15:17–19)

She glanced again at the poster. Straining to reach the back pocket
of her jeans, she pulled out her cell phone and dialed.

"Mom?"

"Janna?"

She blinked hard as tears spilled down her cheeks. "I want to come
home."

Janna's story is true, although I've changed the names and details.
I had the opportunity to meet Rob and Lisa at a writers conference
in South Florida.

"What kept you from losing hope?" I asked Lisa.

"Psalm 40," she said. "When I'd wonder if there was any hope for
Janna, I'd remember David's words. I copied them onto index cards
and plastered them all over the house.

"'He lifted me out of the slimy pit,' she said, "out of the mud and
mire; he set my feet on a rock and gave me a firm place to stand. He
put a new song in my mouth, a hymn of praise to our God. Many will
see and fear the LORD and put their trust in him.'

"I knew if God could do it for David and others like him, He could
do it for my girl. I made Psalm 40 my prayer," she said, her eyes filling with tears. "Every single day of those long five years."

Countless parents, spouses, and loved ones have found similar
hope in God's Word as they've prayed their wayward family members

home. Every book of the Bible pulses with the heartbeat of our Father God for His prodigal children. When we pray to Him on behalf of our loved ones, we rest, confident and secure, that He not only knows our pain, but feels it, too.

More than a sympathetic listener, though, God is an empathetic advocate. As He did with Janna, He can use anything to draw the most rebellious sinner to repentance and faith.

And when they surrender their lives to Him, He'll bring them into a right relationship with himself and with those who love them.

If you're praying for a prodigal, may these truths give you hope.

Take Heart

No matter how deep our loved ones slide into the pit of this world, God can rescue them and draw them to himself.

From the Heart

Father, my heart aches for those I love who are far from you. I long for them to experience the peace, joy, and freedom that come with having a relationship with you. I want them to spend eternity in heaven with you—and with me. When I grow weary and feel tempted to give up hope, remind me how you lifted me and countless others out of the mud and mire, set our feet on the rock of your salvation, and put a new song in our mouths, even praise to you. Strengthen my fearful heart and fill it with hope as I reflect on your Father's heart toward the prodigals we love.

31

He Never Lets Us Go

And you also were included in Christ
when you heard the message of truth,
the gospel of your salvation. When you
believed, you were marked in him with a
seal, the promised Holy Spirit, who is a
deposit guaranteeing our inheritance until
the redemption of those who are God's
possession—to the praise of his glory.

EPHESIANS 1:13–14

"I could give a thousand reasons why I did what I did." Josie lifted sad eyes to meet mine as we sat across the table from each other. "Mike worked a lot, so I spent most of my time home alone with the kids. I was bored—I mean, how many Dr. Seuss books can you read before you want to pull your hair out? I missed my job but knew it was better for the kids if I stayed home with them.

"I never saw it coming," she said softly. "One day a friend from high school messaged me. At first we just talked about old times." She spoke reluctantly as she rubbed her thumb slowly up and down on her iced tea glass. Water drops rolled down the sweating glass like tears. "But then he said he was coming to town on business, and would I like to meet him for coffee?

"I did," she said, "and before long we were sleeping together—me, a pastor's wife. A Bible study teacher. A vacation Bible school leader, for crying out loud." She flung her hands in the air in disgust. "Who does that?"

During the affair, Josie left home and moved in with her new boyfriend, leaving her husband and children devastated.

"It's taken us a very long time to climb out of that hole," she continued. "It was years before I earned back my family's trust. I hurt a lot of people. And I hurt the ministry. But God has been gracious to me."

She brushed her sandy blonde hair from her eyes as if to wipe away the memories, then said with conviction, "One of the most profound aspects of all was how God didn't leave me in my sin. Even when I was running as hard away from Him as I could, He never let me go.

"At night when everything was quiet, I'd hear His voice—convicting me of my choices. *This is wrong. This is not who you are. This won't make you happy.* Sometimes a Bible verse would pop into my head. I started having trouble sleeping."

She took a sip of tea, and a tiny smile tugged at the corners of her mouth. "One day I woke up." She shrugged her shoulders. "I thought about Mike. And the kids. And the life I'd left behind, and God cracked my heart wide open.

"I confessed my sin to God and told Him how sorry I was. Then I called Mike and did the same. I asked him if I could come home.

"I talk with a lot of women who are afraid they've lost their salvation because of their sin," Josie said. "They wonder, 'How could God love me after what I've done?' I tell them, 'Ephesians 1:13–14 tells us, when God saved us, He put His Holy Spirit inside us as a deposit—as proof that He will see us all the way through our lives until He takes us home. He will not let us go, no matter what we do.'"

Today, ten years after her affair, Josie has a powerful ministry. She shares the gospel of salvation to those who have never accepted Christ as Savior, but she also speaks to those who are struggling to persevere in the faith. Every now and then she encounters someone with a story like hers, and they marvel together at how God drew them back, forgave them, and restored them.

"At first, when I came to my senses and saw my sin for what it was, I had a hard time believing God still loved me," Josie said.

She did a deep dive into the Scriptures and found verse after verse reassuring her of God's commitment to those who have genuinely surrendered their lives to God for salvation.

She shares Scripture such as Hebrews 7:25 (emphasis added): "Therefore he is able to *save completely* those who come to God through him, because he *always lives* to intercede for them."

And Ephesians 2:8–9: "For it is by grace you have been saved, through faith—and this is not from yourselves, it is the gift of God—not by works, so that no one can boast."

And John 10:27–29: "My sheep listen to my voice; I know them, and they follow me. I give them eternal life, and they shall never perish; no one will snatch them out of my hand. My Father, who has given them to me, is greater than all; no one can snatch them out of my Father's hand."

Her words and God's irrefutable Word give hope to those who doubt the foreverness of their salvation.

Hearing Josie's story gives me hope, too. I haven't sinned against God and those I love in such a grievous way, but I'll battle my sinful nature until I die. Knowing my heavenly Father will help me persevere and never abandon me, even when I sin against Him, makes me love Him even more.

His commitment to me makes me want to confess my sins quickly so I can live in the fullness of His fellowship again. But even if Satan, the world, or my own flesh deceive me and lure me away, I know God won't abandon me. He'll see me through my trial until it has accomplished its purpose and made me more like His Son. Even my sin can bring Him glory when I surrender it to Him and allow Him to restore me.

The apostle Peter's story, like Josie's, is a tragically beautiful example of God's restoring power. Although Peter failed Christ in His darkest hour by denying that he even knew Him, God drew him back to repentance, restoration, and fruitful ministry. God extends this same saving and preserving power to those of us who sincerely believe.

In this we find hope.

Take Heart

Because God sealed me with His Holy Spirit, I can trust Him to convict me of sin, lead me to repentance, and continue the purifying work He's doing in my life.

From the Heart

Thank you, Father, that there's no sin so grievous a Christian can't repent of it. I'm so grateful your Spirit within us doesn't allow us to remain comfortable with sin but convicts us and woos us back into fellowship. Guard my heart so that I won't sin against you and others. But when I do, help me repent quickly and completely. Create in me a clean heart, oh God, and renew a right spirit within me.

32

God Never Wastes Pain

**We also glory in our sufferings, because
we know that suffering produces
perseverance; perseverance, character;
and character, hope. And hope does not put
us to shame, because God's love has been
poured out into our hearts through the
Holy Spirit, who has been given to us.**

ROMANS 5:3–5

Seven-year-old me decided it would be exhilarating to ride down the slide standing up. Other kids in the schoolyard had done it, and it looked marvelous. With arms extended and hair flying, I mimicked my classmates' smooth sail down the slippery piece of playground equipment. Only for me, it wasn't so slippery. And I didn't sail.

Unlike the curly haired girl in her patent leather Mary Janes who'd gone down ahead of me, I hadn't worn slippery soled shoes. Instead of gliding like a swan on a lake, I tumbled like an armadillo rolling down a hill.

As the ground rose to meet me, I threw out my arms and landed at the bottom in a heap. My breath whooshed from my lungs, leaving me gasping and choking. When I attempted to sit up, pain radiated from my wrist to my elbow. Pinpricks of light flashed before my eyes.

"Go get the teacher," I tried to say to a girl standing nearby. My lips formed the words, but no sound came out. Eventually my breath returned, and I stumbled to my feet. Cradling my right arm, I walked on shaky legs to the school office.

Soon Dad and I were on our way to the doctor's office. X-rays confirmed what the orthopedist suspected—clean breaks in two wrist bones.

"I'd like you to wait outside while I set her arm," he told Dad, nodding toward the door.

Dad smoothed the hair that had fallen over my face and raised my chin until my frightened eyes met his sad ones. "The doctor's going to fix your arm" he said. "I have to wait outside. When it's all bandaged up, I'll be back. Be brave."

I nodded, suppressing my tears. When the door clicked behind him, the doctor took my hand in his and cradled my elbow.

"The broken bones are out of place, and they won't get better unless I fix them. I'm going to pull your arm. It's going to hurt, but it will be over quickly. I promise.

"Ready?"

I nodded again, and the tears that had threatened to fall all afternoon rolled down my cheeks.

Fifty years later, Dad still remembers the scream that echoed down the hallway and into the waiting room. When he mustered the courage to peek into the treatment room, the nurse was applying damp plaster strips to my swollen arm.

I can endure just about any hardship if I know it has a purpose. This is why I cling to Romans 5:3–5 during times of trial: "We also glory in our sufferings, because we know that suffering produces perseverance; perseverance, character; and character, hope. And hope does not put us to shame, because God's love has been poured out into our hearts through the Holy Spirit, who has been given to us."

Paul's seemingly impossible statement that we can *glory* in our sufferings hinges on the promise that they're not meaningless. They accomplish purposes and deliver benefits we never imagine in the midst of them.

I'll be the first to admit I was a spiritual wimp in the early years of my Christian life—as many baby believers are. When the slightest difficulty entered my life, I quaked like an aspen leaf. I whined at hard work. Sacrificial giving, serving, or living held no appeal to me. Like a baby walking on rubbery legs, my spiritual muscles struggled to support me and often sent me tumbling to the ground in a faith crisis heap.

Psalm 34:19 declares: "The righteous person may have many troubles," and it is true.

Challenging work environments hostile to my faith provided opportunities to "work as unto the Lord." Maintaining my Christian witness while my boss mocked my beliefs strengthened my spiritual backbone.

I married and learned what commitment meant. Every day became an opportunity to love, honor, and cherish. Sometimes in sickness. Sometimes in health. Sometimes in poverty. Sometimes in wealth.

Parenting provided a workout for my faith. Colic, separation anxiety, and the teenage years taught me to serve when I didn't feel like serving and give when I didn't feel like giving. I made decisions my children didn't like because it was the right thing to do.

Our family experienced grief, sickness, spiritual valleys, ministry challenges, and prodigal children. Each time we pressed on, we developed perseverance. Circumstances that might have caused us to quit in our early lives inspired us to fortify our faith, ask for help, and double down on our prayers. Our character grew and matured, too. Instead of looking for the easiest way out, we found ourselves volunteering for hard things.

Now that my husband and I have walked with the Lord for forty plus years, we recognize that the times of greatest trial were and are also the times of greatest growth. Hard things press us into God. Hopeless situations humble us. Suffering invites us to examine our lives and root out sin. Afflictions burn the dross from our character and make us more like Christ. As our character deepens, so does our ability to feel hopeful. We no longer doubt God's love, because the Holy Spirit in our hearts confirms it.

While I'd never choose to walk through some of the trials I've experienced, I can rest in confident hope that my suffering isn't useless. God never wastes pain.

Take Heart

Although we don't always understand suffering, we can rest in hope, knowing it's not purposeless. It will accomplish God's good work in our lives.

From the Heart

Oh, Father, what a comfort to know my suffering isn't random. You have a good purpose for everything that filters through your fingers. When my heart aches and my faith trembles, remind me that you are trustworthy and good. Help me look back at the hard times and see how you used them to grow my faith and mature my character. Instead of chafing against trials, help me embrace them in hope. Use them to make me more like Jesus. Amen.

33

God Restores

**You intended to harm me, but God
intended it for good to accomplish what is
now being done, the saving of many lives.**

GENESIS 50:20

Certain Bible verses have the power to change our lives forever. John 3:16 is one, "For God so loved the world that he gave his one and only Son, that whoever believes in him shall not perish but have eternal life." Matthew 28:20 is another, "Surely I am with you always, to the very end of the age."

But what are we to think when our lives are devastated by the deliberate, evil acts of others? Is there a verse (and an accompanying truth) that silences the triumphant shouts of Satan and brings a spiritual perspective to our pain?

There is—Genesis 50:20: "You intended to harm me, but God intended it for good to accomplish what is now being done, the saving of many lives."

This verse, spoken by Joseph, is the crowning glory of the book of Genesis and perhaps one of the most important verses in the Bible.

Despite the fact that Joseph was handsome, honest, and godly (or maybe partly because of it), Joseph's eleven brothers hated him. Jealousy and their father's favoritism moved them to attack him, throw him into a pit, and plot his murder. Trapped at the bottom of that pit, Joseph was no doubt becoming increasingly fearful and losing all hope when a caravan passed by. Joseph's brothers set their murderous plans aside and sold him into slavery instead. The traders marched him off to Egypt, where they auctioned him off to Potiphar, one of Pharaoh's officials.

At first Joseph's circumstances improved. Potiphar recognized his talent and made him overseer of his household. All went well until Mrs. Potiphar cast her adulterous eyes on him. She made her move, but when he resisted and ran, she screamed for help. "This Hebrew has been brought to us to make sport of us!" she said. "He came in here to sleep with me, but I screamed. When he heard me scream for help, he left his cloak beside me and ran out of the house" (Genesis 39:14–15). Her false charges landed Joseph in prison.

Realizing Joseph was no ordinary criminal, the jailer put him in charge of the entire prison. Two of Joseph's fellow prisoners had dreams and Joseph correctly interpreted them. One prisoner was released back into Pharaoh's service but failed to mention Joseph and his innocence, leaving him to languish in jail for two more years. By now, he'd been kidnapped, enslaved, imprisoned, and exiled from his family and his homeland for more than thirteen years.

But Joseph hadn't been exiled from God. Three times in Genesis 39 alone, the Bible tells us, "The Lord was with Joseph" (vv. 2, 21, 23). He was setting the stage for one of the most miraculous deliverances in history.

In God's perfect timing, Joseph was delivered from prison and exalted as Pharaoh's second-in-command. (If you've never read the full story, stop now and read Genesis 37, 39–50.) God enabled him to predict the future and implement a plan to save the country (and his family back in Canaan) from starvation. He reunited with his beloved father and extended forgiveness and restoration to the brothers who wronged him so long ago. As they groveled in fear and shame before him, he spoke the words that somehow make sense of all the wrong they'd done to him.

"You intended to harm me, but God intended it for good to accomplish what is now being done, the saving of many lives" (Genesis 50:20).

These twenty-three words give us an anchor of hope when injustice, evil, and cruelty enter a believer's life. They don't minimize the wrong that's been done against us, nor do they excuse it. God isn't glorified when we sweep wrongdoing under the proverbial rug. Evil is evil. Sin is sinful. Injustice damages everyone it touches.

But God has a greater purpose than anything evil can do to us. He superintends sinful people and their actions with His velvet glove and orders the events of our lives to refine our faith, save the lost, and bring glory to himself.

Christ exists as the perfect example of how God used the evil acts of men to accomplish His glorious work of redemption. Arrested, falsely accused, imprisoned, mocked, beaten, scourged, and crucified, in the fullness of time (Galatians 4:4), Jesus redeemed humankind from the penalty of sin, broke the chains of darkness, and conquered death forever. God allowed every travesty against Christ to bring about His ultimate triumph over evil.

This same God orchestrates the wrong others commit against us to bring about a far greater purpose than our suffering. In His wisdom, goodness, and love, He uses what He hates to accomplish what He loves.

Because of Joseph and because of Jesus, we can trust God with the wrongs others commit against us. We can stand strong in faith because He who promised to care for our souls and redeem our lives is faithful. His nature, which is always good, won't allow anything except what will ultimately accomplish good for us and others. We may not see it now, or even in our lifetimes, but we can trust that, when the time is right, God will stitch every tear, heartbreak, and pain into the tapestry of His perfect plan and purpose.

God lifted Joseph out of the pit and the prison and positioned him to save a nation. He lifted Jesus out of the grave to save the world. We can trust Him to use the wrongs committed against us to ultimately accomplish His glorious purposes.

The apostle Paul, himself a victim of false accusations, beatings, floggings, hunger, thirst, imprisonment, and finally death, called the horrendous acts committed against him "light and momentary troubles" compared to the eternal glory they were accomplishing (2 Corinthians 4:17).

By faith, we too can view our trials in this hope-filled, biblical way. We can rest assured that in God's perfect timing, He will use every one of them to accomplish something beautiful.

Take Heart

In the fullness of time, God will lift you out of the pits and prisons of your life and reveal His glorious purposes.

From the Heart

Father, some days, the only thing that keeps me from losing hope is knowing you will use the evil committed against your children to accomplish a far greater purpose than anything I can see or imagine. When I doubt your character and love, remind me that you are wise and you are good. I can trust you. Amen.

He Empowers Us to Share His Comfort

**Praise be to the God and Father of
our Lord Jesus Christ, the Father of
compassion and the God of all comfort,
who comforts us in all our troubles, so that
we can comfort those in any trouble with
the comfort we ourselves receive from God.**

2 CORINTHIANS 1:3-4

Five women sat around the dining room table at a women's retreat and shared a meal. As they ate, they took turns drawing slips of paper from a plastic cup.

"My icebreaker question is this," the first woman said. "Tell about one of your favorite childhood memories." She told a story about a fun family trip that left us all smiling.

When she finished, the next woman pulled her prompt from the cup and read it aloud. "Tell about a time when you laughed until you cried." She recounted a hilarious story, and we laughed along with her.

Still grinning, my friend Charlotte pulled her prompt from the cup. Her smile faded, and her face grew serious.

She smoothed the strip of crinkled paper and read, "Tell about a time you experienced grief." Taking a deep breath, she squared her shoulders and glanced around the table at the sober faces who waited for her answer. I whispered a prayer for God to give her strength and composure to tell the story I knew was coming.

"On July 2, 2014, at 11:48 p.m. Chicago time, my beautiful, first-born, troubled, twenty-five-year-old daughter ran out onto the Kennedy Expressway in Chicago into the path of an oncoming tractor trailer truck and instantly met Jesus face-to-face."

Any lingering mirth vanished, and a holy hush descended on the room.

"My intent here is not to dwell on the horrific grief and upheaval of my life, but to testify to how the Spirit of God showed up." Sympathetic tears sprang to my eyes as I remembered those horrible first days.

"When I heard the news," Charlotte said, "I was engulfed in a tsunami of grief. But then, a tsunami of grace followed—God's grace." She paused and shook her head slowly, remembering. "I had known in my head His grace was all-sufficient, but I'd never experienced it to this degree. Now it covered, carried, and sustained me.

"On the heels of God's grace," she continued, "I became aware of His comfort—through people who showed up, wrote letters, called, and listened. I discovered, as time went on, that God is not a drive-by comforter. He remains.

"And to this day, almost seven years later, neither His grace nor His comfort have abated." She lowered her head, then raised it again as tears shimmered in her eyes. "I still cry. I still painfully miss my daughter. When I'm alone, I scream out her name. But I am not overcome. I am held by Him until I see her again one day in heaven."

She blinked away tears and continued.

"My first prayer upon receiving the news of our daughter's death was more of a scream. 'God, please don't let Hannah's death be in vain. Redeem this tragedy for Your glory.' Five months later a dear friend lost her son to colon cancer. I was able to speak with her just before he passed away and was able to share with her what to expect—the grief, but more importantly, God's unlimited grace and unending comfort.

"She and I met multiple times over the year after her son's death, and she too was experiencing the presence of the Lord like I had." She paused, then continued. "Did tears fall? Yes. Did heartache still manifest itself? Yes. But she and I knew we were being carried by our heavenly Father through what could have become a valley of despair."

Charlotte slid her plate forward and clasped her hands in front of her. "Since that time, three other women I know have lost a child. I've been able to share with them the reality of God's grace and comfort, which could also be the strength of their lives as they walk through their season of grief."

My friend Charlotte has lived 2 Corinthians 1:3–4. She's experienced the supernatural comfort only God can give, and she's shared that comfort with others facing a similar grief. God has entrusted this particular trial to her, and as she shares her story, uses it to point others to himself.

I pray no one reading this book has experienced the loss of a child, but I suspect some have. Others have walked through the death of a spouse, an extended period of unemployment, a prodigal child, a health crisis, depression, and a myriad of other challenges. God is present to our pain and suffering. Even in the face of our tsunamis of grief, we discover that, no matter what, God won't let us drown.

When we cling to Him, God redeems our suffering and restores our hope. Then He allows us to come alongside another drowning soul, lower the life preserver, and pull them to safety.

"Praise be to the God and Father of our Lord Jesus Christ, the Father of compassion and the God of all comfort, who comforts us in all our troubles, so that we can comfort those in any trouble with the comfort we ourselves receive from God" (2 Corinthians 1:3–4).

Take Heart

When we embrace God's comfort, He restores our hope, redeems our suffering, and comforts others through us.

From the Heart

Father, thank you for providing abundant grace to weather the most treacherous storms. As Charlotte's story reveals, if we open ourselves to you and accept the grace and comfort you offer, our hearts can heal, and our joy can be restored, even if it doesn't feel that way today, or even if I can't imagine what healing could look like right now. Today I offer up to you the painful losses, experiences, and events of my life. Help me receive your comfort and accept the grace you provide to walk through them. Give me the courage to share my story and extend your offer of grace and hope to the people you've appointed to cross my path. In the strong name of Jesus I ask, amen.

God Enables Us to Forgive

> Then Peter came to Jesus and asked, "Lord,
> how many times shall I forgive my brother
> or sister who sins against me? Up to seven
> times?" Jesus answered, "I tell you, not
> seven times, but seventy-seven times."

MATTHEW 18:21-22

An empty, overgrown field languishes where white-bonneted children used to run and play. Gone is the simple building that housed twenty-six children ages six to thirteen. Where learning once blossomed, only dandelions grow.

In October 2006, news from this rural town in central Pennsylvania shocked the world—twice.

First, when Charlie Roberts, a local delivery driver, barricaded himself inside an Amish schoolhouse, took a classroom and its teachers hostage, then released the boys. He systematically shot ten little girls, five of whom died, and then he turned the gun on himself.

Second, when the members of the Amish community—including the parents and grandparents of the murdered children—extended forgiveness to the shooter, his wife, and his family.

On the day Roberts committed his horrendous crime, members of the Nickel Mines community prepared food and delivered it to Roberts' devastated widow. Less than a week after the shooting, families of the children who had died attended Roberts' funeral.

Most of the non-Amish community stayed away, but more than thirty Amish men and women joined the family in silent solidarity. Dressed in the same black mourning garments they'd worn only days before, they formed a semicircle to shield the grieving family from the media. The Old Order Amish voted to divert money from funds that poured in from around the world to the killer's family, even though many victims faced huge medical bills.[1]

Terri Roberts, overwhelmed by the horror of discovering that her son had committed such a heinous crime, remembers how the Amish extended the grace of forgiveness. Henry, a neighbor who served on the board of three of the local Amish schools, made the first overture.

"Henry showed up at our door on Day One, but not without hesitation," she said. "Several times he turned around and went back up the lane, but he felt he was supposed to be there that day."[2]

"We love you," he said. "We don't hold anything against you."[3]

Tears filled Terri's eyes as she remembered. "That just spoke to my husband's heart. . . . It was the first time he had lifted his head that day."[4]

The shooter's wife, Marie, experienced similar forgiveness. Seeking solace at her parents' home, she was perplexed when she noticed Amish men walking their way. Her father went out to meet them. "I saw them put their hand on his shoulder and wrap their arms around him. . . . He told us they had forgiven Charlie, and they were extending grace and compassion over our family."[5]

Terri acknowledges the doubt expressed at the Amish's rapid and countercultural response. "Many felt this forgiveness was too automatic, too quick. The Amish will be the first to say that forgiveness is not easy. Forgiveness, I have learned, is a decision we make. It is not a feeling. Any one of these families would tell you, this has not been an easy road to travel."

Every day they think of five lives senselessly snuffed out. Of five little girls' caskets lying beneath the Pennsylvania soil. Five graduations that never happened, and five weddings that will never be.

They remember and draw hope from Jesus's response to Peter when he asked, "Lord, how many times shall I forgive my brother or sister who sins against me? Up to seven times?"

Jesus answered, "I tell you, not seven times, but seventy-seven times" (Matthew 18:21–22). Then He lived out what He commanded them to do.

"Father, forgive them," He cried from the cross. *I forgive you for the thorns that pierced my brow, the stripes that scourged my back, and the nails that pierced my hands.*

"Forgive them, for they do not know what they are doing" (Luke 23:34).

Only the Spirit of Christ living inside the grieving Amish mothers and fathers enabled them to forgive Charlie Roberts. Only the Spirit of Christ within us enables us to extend similar forgiveness to those who sin against us.

Most of the offenses we experience pale in comparison to the grievous sin Charlie Roberts committed against the Nickel Mines families, but this fact doesn't minimize our pain. The sinful behavior of others affects us in devastating and far-reaching ways.

But regardless of the depth of the sin committed against us, we can have the hope of extending forgiveness through the example of our Lord and Savior, Jesus Christ.

Take Heart

When we think it's impossible to forgive, the Spirit of Christ empowers us to do the impossible.

From the Heart

Father, some days everything within me resists your command to forgive. Instead of extending mercy, I cry for vengeance. Instead of erasing someone's sin debt, I want to shine a spotlight on it. Instead of trusting you to bring about ultimate justice, I yearn to punish those who have sinned against me. Then I remember how, while I was still glorying in my sins, you extended mercy, grace, and forgiveness—and not just then, but every time I ask you for it. Enable me to forgive like you forgive. In Jesus's name I pray, amen.

36

He Gives More Grace

> But he gives more grace.

JAMES 4:6 ESV

When my friend Joyce received a diagnosis of stage II pancreatic cancer, her mind raced in a thousand directions. *My kids. My job. My hair! Chemo, surgery, radiation, nausea. Fifteen percent survival rate after five years.* A single mom, she wondered how (and if) she'd get through the next year of excruciating treatment. And what would happen after that?

When my friend Marilyn lost her husband to a heart attack three days before Christmas, she gathered up the fragments of her life and wondered, *How can I stitch together a new one? How can I face life without my provider, protector, and friend? Will the tears ever stop?*

When my friend Trish received the phone call informing her that her prodigal daughter had been arrested for a DUI—again—she hung her head and wept. *Lord, how can I keep hoping, and praying, and loving this child when I see no evidence that she'll ever change?*

Each of these women—and a multitude more—are shining testimonies to one of the greatest gifts God gives His children—the gift of grace.

We seldom participate in a church service, ministry event, or spiritual conversation without hearing the word *grace*, but what does it mean?

The most common definition we encounter is that of *unmerited favor*. We see it most often expressed in verses like Ephesians 2:8–9: "For it is by grace you have been saved, through faith—and this is not from yourselves, it is the gift of God—not by works, so that no one can boast."

This manifestation of grace acknowledges that we can do nothing within ourselves to merit God's favor or our salvation. We can't earn it through our good works, nor do we deserve it. The grace that extends salvation to those who will believe is one hundred percent God and zero percent humankind.

The second form of grace—the one this devotion spotlights—is *empowering* grace. It's the God-given ability to do supernatural things. Grace is the force behind every movement of humankind for kingdom work.

Listen to Paul speak of this type of grace in his letter to the Corinthian believers: "And God is able to make all grace abound to you, so that having all sufficiency in all things at all times, you will abound in every good work" (2 Corinthians 9:8 ESV). Grace that comes from God empowers us for every task He calls us to do.

Grace has carried Joyce through her cancer journey.

Grace has enabled Marilyn to build a new life without her beloved husband.

Grace has empowered Trish to love her daughter and pray for God's work in her life.

Grace has filled these women with the hope that whatever they face, they will face it with God's mighty power working in them.

When Joyce closed her eyes on the surgical table, not knowing if she'd awaken in recovery or in heaven, God's grace sustained her. When Marilyn walked through the door of her house alone, God's grace wrapped its arms around her. When Trish made the hard choice to let her daughter remain in jail awaiting sentencing, God's grace bolstered her wobbly determination.

"My grace is sufficient for you," Jesus told the apostle Paul as he pleaded with Him for healing, "for my power is made perfect in weakness" (2 Corinthians 12:9).

As we watch our sisters in Christ endure tremendous hardship with courage and faith, we wonder if we would be so strong. What hope do we have to persevere through life's trials without disintegrating into a puddle of fear or abandoning our faith?

We have the same hope they do—that God's grace is sufficient. Regardless of what our future holds, God's grace will be there and will carry us through. His Word, which cannot fail, promises so.

And if circumstances grow beyond what we can humanly endure? God will give us, as James promised the persecuted believers in James 4:6, even "more grace."

In this truth, Joyce, Marilyn, and Trish find great hope, and so can we.

Take Heart

No matter what trial we face, God's grace will enable us to triumph.

From the Heart

Father, sometimes I imagine the most frightening scenarios. And sometimes reality is more frightening than anything I can imagine. Thank you for the hope of ever-present and abundant grace. Knowing your grace will enable me to face whatever you allow into my life bolsters my faltering courage and calms my fears. Thank you for providing everything I need, every time I need it. In Jesus's name I pray, amen.

37

He Sees and Remembers Our Work

God is not unjust; he will not
forget your work and the love you
have shown him as you have helped his
people and continue to help them.

HEBREWS 6:10

High on a hill in the center of Arlington National Cemetery sits one of the most revered American landmarks, the Tomb of the Unknown Soldier. Although servicemen and women have been buried in Arlington since the Civil War, the monument was inspired by the multitudes of unknown dead in World War I. These soldiers were buried where they fell—far from their homeland—in hastily dug graves in Great Britain and France.

The inaugural burial for the original Unknown Soldier took place at Arlington National Cemetery in 1921. In 1956, President Dwight D. Eisenhower signed a bill into law to pay tribute to unknown soldiers from World War II and the Korean War at this venerated place. Each year, millions visit the Tomb of the Unknown Solder. The tombstone, completed in 1932, reads, "Here rests in honored glory an American soldier known but to God."

The tomb has remained guarded at all times since 1937. On April 6, 1948, the Third US Infantry Regiment took over the mission. A highly trained sentinel stands watch 24 hours a day, 7 days a week, 365 days a year.

These soldiers, elite members of the Old Guard, embody the military's commitment to memorialize those who fought and died in service to our country. For more than seventy years, these men (and a few women) have kept watch—on holidays; at night; and during blizzards, hurricanes, and freezing temperatures.

Although they receive permission, during extreme weather conditions, to retreat to a sheltered area in full view of the tomb, few avail themselves of this option. They prefer to march—twenty-one steps across the mat in front of the grave markers, then twenty-one steps back—with the precision of a metronome, until they are relieved by the next sentinel.

In September 2003, while Hurricane Isabel ripped through the nation's capital with wind gusts of almost sixty miles per hour, the soldiers remained at their post. In 2017, the Old Guard stood watch over the tomb during Hurricane Irene. Although the cemetery was closed to visitors during the COVID-19 pandemic, sentinels continued to guard the tomb.

Captain Harold Earls, one of the soldiers on duty, told CBS affiliate WUSA9, "It's important to show this country that we haven't forgotten."[6]

Most of us have never defended our country in military service, but if we're children of God, we've pledged our allegiance to a kingdom and an army far greater than anything this world has ever seen. We don't wrestle against a flesh-and-blood enemy. We engage in spiritual warfare against the spiritual forces of evil attempting to penetrate and destroy our homes, families, churches, communities, and nations (Ephesians 6:12).

We fight in the trenches of difficult marriages, struggling churches, and fractured families. We pray outside abortion clinics and help the poor, homeless, and sick. We stand for right even when it costs us, champion biblical truth, and train our children to know and love God. We fight spiritual battles with weapons of faith, love, and prayer.

We log countless hours and thousands of steps chasing toddlers, training teenagers, and caring for the sick and the elderly. No one sees us (or so we think) as we wipe that child's nose for the hundredth time or change a thousand stinky diapers. No one hears us patiently answer the same question ten times from our preschooler or our Alzheimer's-compromised parent. When we love and respect our spouse, not because they deserve it, but because God commands it, no one awards us a medal or recognizes our devotion.

We feel unknown as we serve in ways that appear menial and insignificant, but God's Word says otherwise. "God is not unjust," Hebrews 6:10 assures us. "He will not forget your work and the love you have shown him as you have helped his people and continue to help them."

The testimony of Scripture confirms we are not forgotten or unknown. God sees every kind act, selfless sacrifice, and whispered prayer prompted by our love for Him. We can persevere, knowing God not only sees our service on His behalf, but, one day, will reward it with a far greater tribute than a sentinel, a wreath, and a headstone.

The men and women who guard the Tomb of the Unknown Soldier remind us that our country hasn't forgotten those who dedicated their lives to serve our country. Hebrews 6:10 reminds us God hasn't forgotten us. Because of this, we can have hope.

Take Heart

God promises He'll never forget the work we've done or the love we've shown to others.

From the Heart

Father, it comforts me to know that even when I feel unseen, you see me. If no one says thank you or acknowledges my efforts, knowing that you see them helps me press on. Give me your strength to persevere and help me not lose heart. In Jesus's name I pray, amen.

38

He Will Reward Our Sacrifices

**And everyone who has left houses or brothers
or sisters or father or mother or wife or children
or fields for my sake will receive a hundred
times as much and will inherit eternal life.**

MATTHEW 19:29

Carlos and Sandy Rios and Scot and Carol Musser are career missionaries. Carlos and Sandy serve in Mexico. Scot and Carol minister in Spain. If you add up their years of service, they've invested more than one hundred twenty years in God's kingdom.

When their friends studied engineering and banking, they learned cross-cultural evangelism and a second language. When classmates sent out resumes to Fortune 500 companies, they applied to mission boards. When young adults in their circles reviewed benefit packages and 401(k) plans, they raised support to go on the mission field.

During their thirty plus years as expatriates, they've raised and educated their children in foreign countries, sent their high school graduates back to the United States for college, and lived thousands of miles away as their children studied, dated, and married.

They've missed countless family gatherings, weddings, and funerals. When a family member died, they grieved from afar. When their grandchildren were born, they lived oceans away. They've never attended Grandparents Day or picked up their grandchildren from kindergarten. They've never lived in one place longer than ten years.

Not a very rosy picture of missionary life, is it?

Yet if you ask them, knowing what a life of full-time missionary service has cost them, if they'd make the same decision again, they answer with a resounding yes.

They've experienced the joy of seeing men, women, and children place their faith in Christ and grow in their faith. They've planted churches and a school that preaches and teaches the Bible and evangelizes the lost. They've been used of God to help restore broken marriages, families, and lives. They've witnessed God do great and mighty works that defy human explanation. They've served as the hands, feet, and heart of Jesus to a lost and dying world.

Carlos and Sandy and Scot and Carol say, with the apostle Paul, "But whatever were gains to me I now consider loss for the sake of Christ" (Philippians 3:7).

"Missionaries are my heroes," my husband often says, and I agree. But missionaries aren't the only heroes. They're not the only ones who sacrifice for Jesus. We do, too.

"Ordinary" believers who live sold-out lives for Christ suffer loss every day. We offer up our time, talent, and treasure to God's work. We serve others when we'd rather serve ourselves. We yield our rights and preferences for the good of the kingdom. We speak the truth and stand for what's right, even when it costs us something. We offer our bodies as living sacrifices for God to do His work through us.

Christ-followers, whether they're full-time missionaries or sold-out laypeople, die to themselves daily so God might be glorified.

If we're living for God, what hope does God offer when the losses seem to outweigh the gains? Is it really worth it to serve God?

Bold and brash Peter was the only disciple who dared to ask Jesus this question, the one all the others were thinking. "We have left everything to follow you! What then will there be for us?" (Matthew 19:27).

What, indeed?

"Truly I tell you," Jesus said, "at the renewal of all things, when the Son of Man sits on his glorious throne, you who have followed me will also sit on twelve thrones, judging the twelve tribes of Israel. And everyone who has left houses or brothers or sisters or father or mother or wife or children or fields for my sake will receive a hundred times as much and will inherit eternal life" (vv. 28–29).

What a promise. A hundred times reward *and* eternal life. While the right to sit on twelve thrones applies only to the disciples, the promise of heavenly rewards that far outweigh our earthly sacrifices extends to everyone who has suffered loss for the sake of Christ.

"Whatever you do, work at it with all your heart," Paul encouraged the believers in Colossae, "as working for the Lord, not for human masters, since you know that you will receive an inheritance from the Lord as a reward" (Colossians 3:23–24).

"Look, I am coming soon!" Jesus promised in Revelation 22:12, "My reward is with me, and I will give to each person according to what they have done."

These and many other promises give us solid hope that God not only sees the work we do in His name, He'll one day reward us in eternity.

Has it cost you to serve Jesus? If not, are you playing it too safe? It's not too late. You don't have to be a missionary like the Rioses and the Mussers to earn the rewards God promises. The five-talent steward who served his master well received the same reward as the ten-talent steward. "Well done, good and faithful servant! You have been faithful with a few things; I will put you in charge of many things. Come and share your master's happiness!" (Matthew 25:21).

If you've ever wondered if serving God is worth it, take hope. Someday soon you'll receive a great reward. "'What no eye has seen, what no ear has heard, and what no human mind has conceived'—the things God has prepared for those who love him" (1 Corinthians 2:9).

It will be worth it all.

Take Heart

God not only sees the sacrifices we make on His behalf, He promises to reward them.

From the Heart

Oh, Father, some days (most days) the Christian life is hard. I struggle to give, and serve, and love unselfishly. I forget that you promise to reward those who faithfully serve you. I act like this world is all there is and it's up to me to look out for myself. Remind me that a far greater reward awaits me that will outshine anything I give up for you. I love you, Lord Jesus. I really do.

39

He Draws Near

**Come near to God and he
will come near to you.**

JAMES 4:8

When someone in my household succumbs to a virus, infection, or other malady, I reach for the Lysol. Most children associate chicken soup and ginger ale with childhood illnesses, but not mine. They recall the scent of Lysol every time.

Once I've launched a suffocating cloud of disinfecting spray, I grab the germ-killing wipes. With the precision of a special ops team, I swoop in and wipe down everything that doesn't have skin, fabric, or fur. What can't be wiped down and isn't alive goes into the washing machine, where I scald the offending germs in a tub of hot water and bleach.

I isolate the patient in a room by themselves; provide food, drinks, and medication; and check on them periodically. Before COVID-19,

I'd hold my breath when I entered the room. Now I just slap on a handy-dandy N95 and charge in.

The sickie remains in quarantine until their temperature returns to normal and all bodily eruptions have ceased.

I'm not coldhearted or neglectful, just cautious. I credit my first-born, take-charge nature and forty years of infection-control training.

My husband, David, the baby of four siblings, is trained in pastoral care instead of germ prevention. He takes a very different approach. He gathers our grandbabies into his arms and lets them cough into his shoulder. He snuggles them in the La-Z-Boy and watches movies with them. He charges into the sick house with nary a mask in sight to deliver popsicles and Pedialyte.

His fearless, big-hearted approach became intensely personal the day I succumbed to the flu. Fever caused me to alternate between shivering and sweating. Coughing spasms rendered conversation impossible. Body aches made me feel like a squirrel who'd crossed the Daytona racetrack without looking both ways.

As I gathered my pillow and blanket and prepared to sequester myself in the guest room, David's voice stopped me.

"Don't go. Sleep here tonight. I'll snuggle you, and you'll feel better."

In my weakened state, I forgot every single infection-control protocol I'd learned. I crawled between the covers and allowed my warm, comforting husband to wrap me in his soft embrace. David modeled God's heart toward believers who are sin sick and helpless.

Instead of turning away from us when we turn toward Him, God opens His arms and welcomes us in. James 4:8 records His words. "Draw near to God, and he will draw near to you" (ESV).

Unfortunately, when we've disobeyed His Word and sickened ourselves with the yuck of this world, we often avoid drawing near to God. We turn our faces from Him because we know our sin is offensive. We refuse to admit we need His healing, cleansing touch. Sometimes we run from Him, reveling in our disobedience and blind to how much we need Him.

The prodigal son in Luke 15 exemplifies both our sinfulness and God's loving-kindness. He grew up in his father's house and enjoyed a relationship with him but chose to pursue the pleasures of sin for a season. His choices broke his father's heart, but the father let him go.

Yet every day he watched and longed for his son to return.

My husband could have turned away from me because my sickness made me repulsive. Instead, he chose to welcome me into his loving embrace. God does the same. He won't chase after us, but as the father did with his prodigal son, He'll welcome us back into His love. When we repent and return to Him, He gathers up His holy robes and runs to embrace us.

With a smile that parts the heavens, He wraps His strong arms around us, kisses our tearstained faces, and rouses the family to celebrate. "This son of mine was dead and is alive again; he was lost and is found" (Luke 15:24).

Sometimes, I'm sad to admit, I turn away from the Father who loves me best. The ravages of sin sickness—bitterness, faithlessness, independence, selfishness, and disobedience—make me think I'm too distasteful for Him to welcome me back. But God's Word says otherwise. "Draw near to God," the Bible promises, "and he will draw near to you" (James 4:8 ESV).

Is there a sin in your life that keeps you from your loving Father? Confess it. Forsake it. Fall into God's embrace.

Take Heart

God, our faithful Father, welcomes us back into fellowship with open arms and a forgiving heart.

From the Heart

Father, your tender, forgiving, never-ending love for me never ceases to amaze me. Even when my sinful actions or attitudes make you sad, you never stop loving me. Thank you for not allowing me to remain in my sin, but for lovingly and persistently calling me back to yourself. Time and time again you convict me of my sins, move me to confess, and welcome me back into sweet fellowship with you. Thank you, precious Savior, amen.

40

God Will Sustain Us in Our Old Age

Even to your old age and gray hairs
I am he, I am he who will sustain you.
I have made you and I will carry you; I will
sustain you and I will rescue you.

ISAIAH 46:4

For almost forty years, I've listed my official occupation as *registered dental hygienist*, but if you examined the early years of my life, I spent most of my time as a *professional worrier*. An anxious firstborn who loved to control everything, I worried about what could happen, what had happened, and what didn't happen. I fretted about the future, the past, and the present. I'd lie awake nights imagining terrifying possibilities and dreadful prospects.

Childhood invited the boogeyman to live under my bed. Adolescence blossomed with physical, emotional, and social angst. Young adulthood swarmed with a host of life-impacting decisions.

Then I surrendered my life to Christ.

As I learned to navigate life as a Christian, I continued to find reasons to worry, but I also discovered reasons to trust. When I developed the habit of Bible reading, I learned the character and nature of God. Soon, my pile of reasons to trust God towered over the heap of reasons I had to fear.

As I move through my adult years, I've discovered that every new season invites new anxiety. I watch my parents and other "senior saints" age and decline in health, and I wonder about my twilight years. Will I trust God until the end?

To keep my heart steadfast and hope filled, I must continually guard it and revisit the reasons God gives us to trust and not be afraid. Like rose petals on a wedding aisle, the Bible's promises are strewn throughout Scripture. They are promises we can cling to. One of my favorites in this season of life is the promise God gave his people in Isaiah 46:4: "Even to your old age and gray hairs I am he, I am he who will sustain you. I have made you and I will carry you; I will sustain you and I will rescue you." Because I'm one of His children, this promise applies to me, too.

In my decades as a Christian, I've gotten to know senior saints and have watched God's faithfulness displayed in their lives. Seeing God's tender care for them gives me hope for my own latter years.

Ninety-five-year-old Lairy Easterling began every prayer with the same words, "Thank you, Lord, for this beautiful world you have given us." He worked hard all his life and lived modestly in a two-bedroom bungalow in a neighborhood that had seen better days.

Although he lost an eye in a work accident and buried his only son, he never missed an opportunity to testify how God had faithfully provided for him and his wifev Nell, all the days of their lives.

Ninety-two-year-old Elmer Thompson and his wife, Evelyn, also beautifully demonstrated God's steadfast love and care during their many years on Earth. The cofounder of West Indies Mission (now TEAM), Elmer often testified how God met their needs in unexpected and miraculous ways. Their path wasn't smooth or pain free, but every step they took had God's fingerprints on it.

God protected them when they were ejected from Cuba after Fidel Castro rose to power. He met their needs as they traveled the country to recruit new candidates for their mission. He surrounded them with a physical and a faith family in their final years. Whenever he had the opportunity to speak, Elmer began with the words, "God has been good to me."

These modern-day men took their cue from the patriarchs. Jacob, on his deathbed, testified of "the God who has been my shepherd all my life to this day, the Angel who has delivered me from all harm" (Genesis 48:15–16). King David observed, "I was young and now I am old, yet I have never seen the righteous forsaken or their children begging bread" (Psalm 37:25). The prophet Jeremiah, who witnessed the destruction of his beloved Jerusalem, declared, "Blessed is the one who trusts in the LORD, whose confidence is in him" (Jeremiah 17:7).

Strangely enough, I take my greatest comfort from the story of Lazarus in Luke 16. Covered with sores and begging at a rich man's gate, he seemed to contradict David's observation that he'd never seen "the righteous forsaken or their children begging bread." In the story, even Abraham agreed that Lazarus's final days were difficult, acknowledging to the rich man, "in your lifetime you received your good things, while Lazarus received bad things" (Luke 16:25).

I'm sure Lazarus would have preferred God meet his needs in more dignified ways and bless him with soundness of body until he died peacefully in his sleep, but his life, too, proves God's faithfulness. Scripture tells us God provided someone to carry him to the rich man's gate. He fed him through others' generosity. Best of all, He dispatched a contingent of angels to usher him from this world to the next, where he rested, safe and satisfied, in God's presence forever.

I don't know what my final years on Earth will look like. If I get to choose, I'll vote for creature comforts, health, and a padded 401(k). If I possess none of these and live like a modern-day Lazarus, however, God's promises are still true. "Even to your old age and gray hairs I am he, I am he who will sustain you. I have made you and I will carry you; I will sustain you and I will rescue you" (Isaiah 46:4).

Take Heart

We can face our twilight years with hope. God will sustain us.

From the Heart

Thank you, Father, for your faithfulness to the aged. This gives me great hope. No matter what happens in my future, I know you'll take care of me. When I feel afraid, remind me of your history of faithfulness to your children. Grow my trust in you.

Part 3

God's Word
(What God Says)

41

God's Word Always Accomplishes His Purpose

So is my word that goes out from my mouth: It will not return to me empty, but will accomplish what I desire and achieve the purpose for which I sent it.

ISAIAH 55:11

When Carlos Gomez was sixteen years old, a man climbed four flights of stairs to the apartment in Spain where he and his mother lived and knocked on the door. When she opened it, he handed her a Bible.

"This is a gift for you," he said, and then he was gone.

At the time, Spain was ruled by Francisco Franco, a dictator who forbade all but a few token churches. Bibles were outlawed. Even the Catholic priests didn't have them.

But now Carlos's mother did.

Curious, she began to read. And something happened.

"She came alive inside," Carlos said. "And then she began to pray for me. I'd hear her at night in the small bedroom we shared, when I pretended to be asleep."

His mother prayed, "Lord, open his eyes. Make the Bible real to him, too."

Carlos resisted his mother's urgings to read the Bible for himself, but he couldn't deny the transformation taking place in her life. "One night after she'd gone to bed, I picked up her Bible. I read it all night long," he remembers. "When morning came and my mother awoke, I was still reading.

"She knew her prayers had been answered."

Carlos repented of his sin and surrendered his life to Christ. Gradually, the same Bible that had transformed his mother transformed him.

Hebrews 4:12 describes the power of the Scriptures: "For the word of God is alive and active. Sharper than any double-edged sword, it penetrates even to dividing soul and spirit, joints and marrow; it judges the thoughts and attitudes of the heart."

In the months following Carlos's and his mother's conversions, they wondered how many of their neighbors had also received Bibles from the mysterious stranger. One by one they quizzed those who lived in their building. They described the man and asked if he had also knocked on their door. They soon realized only Carlos's mother had received a visit or a Bible.

"Why did he climb four flights of stairs to knock on our door and give my mother a Bible?" Carlos still wonders. The man shared no gospel presentation, nor did he leave pamphlets or evangelical material. Just the Bible.

"It was enough," Carlos says with a shrug. "God's Word always accomplishes God's purpose."

Believers down through the ages have always shared God's Word. Isaiah and other faithful prophets took God's message to their fellow Israelites. Jesus taught in the synagogues from the Old Testament Scriptures. Peter preached the word to the Jews, and 5,000 people came to faith in Christ (Acts 4:4). Billy Graham shared the Word with an estimated 2.2 billion people, resulting in 2.2 million conversions through his crusades.[1]

And one unnamed man climbed four flights of stairs to deliver one Bible to one woman who accepted Christ and shared her Bible with her son.

To date, Carlos and his family have planted six evangelical churches in Spain and have teamed up with locals to start seventeen more. Carlos's goal is to start churches in towns where there are no believers. His teams survey the population to discover their needs, share the gospel, and, of course, hand out Bibles.

Whether we distribute thousands of Bibles on college campuses like the Gideons or write a carefully chosen Bible verse in a card, we can be hope filled, knowing God's Word will never return void. It will always accomplish the purpose God intends for it.

Take Heart

However we share God's Word, we can be confident it will never return void. It always accomplishes His good purposes.

From the Heart

Father, sometimes I grow discouraged. I feel like I can't make a difference. Thank you for the hope of Isaiah 55:11. Help me continue to share your Word in a bold yet winsome way with those around me. Remind me that my responsibility is to obey your prompting. Your job is to apply it to their lives. In Jesus's precious name I pray, amen.

42

Hope When You Feel Small

Who dares despise the day of small things?

ZECHARIAH 4:10

"There it is," my friend Kim said. "My favorite house on the lake."

We were boating along the shores of Lake Murray in Gilbert, South Carolina, in her pontoon boat, when Kim turned into a cove and cut the engine. As we drifted toward shore, she pointed to a home dead center at the back of the cove.

We'd already sailed past three-story columned homes graced with palmetto trees, plantation-style houses with perfectly manicured lawns and flowering crepe myrtles, and ultra-modern structures with large windows overlooking the water.

I expected her favorite house to be a mansion. Or a design masterpiece. What she pointed to, however, looked like a boathouse.

Wedged in between two palatial structures, the tiny home sat in the middle of a patch of grass like an egg in an Easter basket. The house boasted about a thousand feet of living space.

And it was lovely. A shiny copper roof sat atop a simple brick exterior. Flowers and a stone path wound from the house to the water. Like a teenager who'd just gotten her braces off, a fancy front door smiled proudly from its front. A sign hung from a wrought-iron post at the edge of the water. In big black letters and all caps, it read, SMALL.

I assume Small is the name of the tiny house's owners, but I can't help wondering if the sign has a double meaning. In my mind, the sign declares, I'm small, and I'm okay with that. I'm not trying to be something I'm not or wishing I were different. I'm celebrating what I am with no apologies.

I wish I could embrace the smallness of my existence as confidently as the Small house does. Sometimes I chafe at my small impact, small church, small platform, and small life. Thousands of small tasks fill my days, and I wonder if any of them matter at all.

When I grow discouraged, the words of Zechariah 4 give me hope. "The hands of Zerubbabel have laid the foundation of this temple; his hands will also complete it. Then you will know that the LORD Almighty has sent me to you. Who dares despise the day of small things . . . ?" (vv. 9–10).

As Zerubbabel led the newly returned exiles to rebuild the temple, young people rejoiced, and old people wept. The senior members of the community remembered Solomon's palatial temple structure. Compared to this, Zerubbabel's temple would look like a mobile home.

God understood their grief, but He reminded them that He often uses small people doing small tasks to accomplish His great work.

He called one man, Noah, to build an ark and save the human race from destruction (Genesis 6:13–19).

He used Abraham, an old man with a barren wife, to birth the nation of Israel (Isaiah 51:2). He called the Israelites to be obedient to the simple task of marching around the walls of an impenetrable city so He could overtake Jericho on their behalf (Joshua 6).

He used Ruth, a converted Moabite, who willingly served her grieving mother-in-law, to continue the family line of Christ (Ruth 2:11–12).

He anointed the youngest son of Jesse to lead the nation as king (1 Samuel 16:10–12). (And before David became a leader, God called him to the ordinary, daily responsibility of caring for a flock of sheep to help ready him to become Israel's shepherd.)

He used a housewife with a jug of milk and a tent peg to kill the commander of the invading army (Judges 4:21).

He brought forth the Messiah from a tiny embryo implanted into the womb of a willing young woman from the obscure town of Nazareth (Matthew 1:18).

When Jesus was grown, He commended the widow's willingness to give all she had, a tiny mite (Mark 12:42–44) and fed a multitude with a small boy's lunch (John 6:9–11).

He entrusted the mysteries of the kingdom of heaven to a small band of men (Matthew 28:16–20) and enables ordinary people like you and me to share the good news of the gospel to all who will listen (Matthew 24:14).

When I lose hope and wonder if God can use my small gifts to advance His kingdom, I remember His words to the Israelites: "Who dares despise the day of small things?" (Zechariah 4:10).

Who indeed.

Take Heart

God specializes in using small acts of obedience to accomplish great things in His kingdom.

From the Heart

Father, sometimes I don't feel very gifted or useful. Much of my days are spent doing small tasks that don't seem to matter much in light of eternity. Whenever I feel insignificant and lose hope, remind me of the way you've used the obedient acts of faithful believers down through the ages to glorify your name and point others to yourself.

43

We Are His People

**Know that the Lord is God. It is he who
made us, and we are his; we are his people,
the sheep of his pasture.**

PSALM 100:3

If I asked you who your people are, what would you say?

The first thing that comes to most of our minds is family. Whether or not we agree on everything, live nearby, or hang out just for fun, we know our people are there for us. We can call them when a health crisis threatens, one of our kids is in trouble, or we need help dealing with crazy Aunt Mary. Our shared history and DNA link us in ways that transcend personality and preference.

My husband often says of his big brother, Luther, "He'd beat me up, but if anyone else tried to mess with me, I knew he'd have my back." My relationship with my sister Tina is much less physical, but whenever I need her, she's there. She's my people.

Friends sit at the top of the list of *my people*. These women (you know who you are) pray for me and with me, share my adventures, and weep with me when my heart is broken. They say hard things because they love me and cheer me on when I grow discouraged.

My friends have babysat my children at a moment's notice, brought food when I had the flu, and ministered beside me in a foreign country. They bring me chocolate at all the right times and never judge. I can share my deep dark secrets and know they're safe.

Not everyone has family and friends like these who will stand beside them. Maybe your family is fractured into a thousand pieces, and you haven't spoken to your parents or siblings in years. You might have friends who failed you when you needed them most. I've been there, too.

Maybe this devotion has made you feel sad and lonely. Maybe even hopeless, because you're wondering who, if anyone, is *your people*.

God inspired Psalm 100:3 for times like these. "Know that the LORD is God. It is he who made us, and we are his; *we are his people*, the sheep of his pasture" (emphasis added).

Don't you love this? God calls us His people. We belong to Him. When He saves us, He puts us into His family. He's our Father, and we are His kids. Stronger than blood, friendship, or preference, His love and commitment bind us to Him forever.

He won't abandon us, nor will He turn a deaf ear to our cries. Every time we call His name, He hears and answers. "The LORD is near to all who call on him," the psalmist testified, "to all who call on him in truth" (Psalm 145:18).

Even when we break His heart, He never locks us out. He's a forgiving Father. As soon as we turn our feet toward home in confession and repentance, He flings the front door open wide. "Come near to God," James 4 promises, "and he will come near to you. . . . Humble yourselves before the Lord, and he will lift you up" (vv. 8, 10).

Because of Jesus, my Savior and my Shepherd, God Almighty has adopted me into His fold. "I am the good shepherd," Jesus said. "I know my sheep and my sheep know me" (John 10:14). We know His voice, and He knows ours. We can always draw near to God.

We are safe. Secure. Loved. We can have hope because *we are His people.*

Take Heart

We will always have a place of belonging because we are God's people.

From the Heart

Father, thank you so much for welcoming me into your family and calling me your own. What a privilege. When I feel lonely and abandoned, remind me that I belong to you, and you'll never turn me away. When I feel like no one loves me, remind me that you love me with an everlasting love. Thank you for making me, saving me, and welcoming me into your family as one of your people.

44

We Have a Living Hope

**Praise be to the God and Father of
our Lord Jesus Christ! In his great mercy
he has given us new birth into a living
hope through the resurrection of
Jesus Christ from the dead.**

1 PETER 1:3

My grandmother's green thumb was legendary. She once planted a fence post and grew a tree.

A Portuguese immigrant who came to the United States during World War I, Granny loved planting gardens and growing plants. A collection of houseplants filled a sunny spot in her living room, and a small garden supplied vegetables for her family.

Money was scarce, so she learned to make do with whatever materials she had on hand. One day, attempting to keep rabbits out of her garden, she built a makeshift fence out of tree limbs she found on the side of the road. The long, straight branches from a neighbor's pruning project made ideal anchors for the chicken wire she strung around her plot.

Granny's efforts succeeded. No bunnies munched her lettuce. When spring arrived the next year, she checked her fence for breaks and prepared to plant. To her surprise, fuzzy white buds covered the fence sticks. Her seemingly lifeless fencing material had become a vibrant pussy willow border.

She performed the same magic, minus the chicken wire, on a vine she pinched from a friend's string of hearts plant. She placed the three-inch strand of heart-shaped leaves into a juice glass until spidery roots appeared, then planted it in a chipped teacup. Within months the vine had crept over the teacup rim and trailed across the windowsill.

When my mom admired the plant, Granny pinched off a piece, wrapped it in a damp paper towel, and sent it home with detailed instructions. Months later I admired Mom's new plant and returned home with a snip of my own.

Two decades after my granny died, a cutting from the string of hearts plant she rooted occupies the sunny spot on my windowsill. When my daughter, now grown with a home and family of her own, admired the dainty plant, I told her the story. Pinching off a piece, I wrapped it in a damp paper towel and sent her home with detailed instructions.

Peter the apostle shared Christ with Jews and Gentiles living in and around Jerusalem. When he and other disciples shared the truth of the gospel with those around them, they perpetuated the faith, causing it to root, grow, and spread.

The life of the gospel—like Granny's string of hearts plant—was passed along and sustained, transcending any one person or generation.

When persecution came, the believers scattered throughout the northern regions of Asia Minor. Peter wrote the epistle of 1 Peter to encourage them.

"Praise be to the God and Father of our Lord Jesus Christ! In his great mercy he has given us new birth into a living hope through the resurrection of Jesus Christ from the dead" (1 Peter 1:3).

A living hope.

What a beautiful description of "an inheritance that can never perish, spoil or fade . . . kept in heaven for you" (v. 4).

The pagan religions of the surrounding nations offered only empty promises based on dead gods, but Christianity promised a living hope. This faith was rooted in Jesus, who had lived a perfect life, died a sacrificial death, and rose again to prove He had conquered the grave.

Our family plant has survived for four generations, but one day it may pass to someone who won't value or nurture it. The plant could weaken with age. A careless owner might forget to water it or subject it to harsh conditions. Without the proper care, it could die.

The living hope of our faith, however, can't be damaged by evil or destroyed by death. It's sin-proof and age-proof. If we've repented of our sins and placed our faith in Christ for our salvation, it cannot fail. God guards and preserves it in heaven for us.

Because it is a living hope, the inheritance God has perpetuated through a string of believing hearts down through the ages is wholly secure and fully alive. Past, present, and future, it grows and spreads until God gathers us all to be with Him in heaven forever.

Take Heart

Because Christ is alive, our hope is, too.

From the Heart

Oh, Father, what a comfort to know that the hope that comes through Jesus's death, burial, and resurrection is as alive as He is. Because He triumphed over death, hell, and the grave, we can, too. What a joy it is to know we serve a living Savior.

45

We'll See Our Babies in Heaven

Can I bring him back again? I will go to him, but he will not return to me.

2 SAMUEL 12:23

For about ten years, I was the firstborn in my family. My parents loved, affirmed, and celebrated me, and my place at the front of their string of daughters was unquestioned.

Then I learned I had a brother.

I grew up being referred to as "The Miracle Baby." I assumed the name came about because of the surgery Mom had when she was seven-months pregnant with me. Doctors knew a lot less in the 1960s about performing operations on pregnant women, but they knew enough to warn my parents I might be born blind or deaf. Or enter the world prematurely. Or not survive at all.

When I arrived full term, healthy, and in possession of all my senses, they celebrated. I grew up in the glow of love-filled, grateful hearts.

Then one day, my sister asked my visiting grandmother how many grandchildren she had. Because she had ten children and all ten had children, she ran out of fingers to count on. She took out a piece of paper and began a list. When she got to our branch of the family tree, she counted me, my sister Cindy, my sister Tina, and "your brother."

My brother?

Until that day, my family had never mentioned I had a brother. And that he died three days after his birth. Born oxygen-deprived and brain-damaged, Robert Wayne Slice died just two weeks after my parents' first wedding anniversary. Mom was eighteen years old.

Today's culture is very different from that of yesteryear. People seldom talked about stillborn, miscarried, or premature babies. There were no support groups or literature. These tiny babies vanished as if they'd never existed. Families seldom held funerals.

My brother was buried in an unmarked grave beside my great-grandmother in the local cemetery. Within six weeks, the grass had grown back over the square of soil that covered his casket, hiding forever the fact that a tiny boy with dark hair and blue eyes rested there.

In the days that followed my grandmother's revelation, I mourned the brother I'd never known. What ten-year-old in an all-girl family didn't imagine how wonderful it would be to have a handsome older brother to protect her? And then to find out that I had, indeed, had one? I grieved deeply for the things that could have been.

Years later, after I came to faith in Christ, I read the story of David and Bathsheba's son who died in infancy. During the seven days of the baby's illness, David fasted and prayed. When his servants brought word that the child had died, in 2 Samuel 12:23, David spoke words that have brought hope and peace to generations of grieving families. "I will go to him, but he will not return to me."

I will go to him.

His words are our words, too, as we grieve the loss of aborted and stillborn babies, infants, and children too young to place their faith in Christ for salvation. One day, because we have trusted in Jesus and accepted His gift of eternal life, we will see them again.

I find great hope in knowing that the brother I never met has spent the past fifty years safe in the arms of Jesus. I don't know if he has a physical body or a spiritual one, a childlike one or a mature one, but I can picture the scene Matthew described when Christ was on the earth. Jesus called a child to His side and lifted Him onto his knee.

"See that you do not despise one of these little ones," He said. "For I tell you that their angels in heaven always see the face of my Father in heaven. . . . In the same way your Father in heaven is not willing that any of these little ones should perish" (Matthew 18:10, 14).

Where is God when we grieve the loss of tiny infants and children? Weeping with us. As He did at the grave of Lazarus, He joins us in our sorrow, lamenting the devastation and loss sin has caused on the earth.

I wonder, as He stood outside Lazarus's grave, if He looked back toward the garden of Eden where He created Adam's and Eve's eternal souls and whispered, "I created mankind to live forever—and one day you will. Until then, we'll weep and mourn together."

To us, He issues both a warning and an invitation. "Unless you change and become like little children [simple, trusting, faith filled], you will never enter the kingdom of heaven" (Matthew 18:3).

But if we do, we'll spend forever with Jesus and the babies who have gone on before us. We'll live in their presence not just for a lifetime, but for all eternity.

In this our grieving hearts find hope.

Take Heart

While we grieve the loss of children in this life, we have hope that we'll spend eternity with them in the next.

From the Heart

Father, there's nothing harder to bear than the death of a child. Thank you for the assurance you gave David that is also ours to claim—that one day we will see our babies again. Until that day, comfort our grieving hearts as only you can do. You were a Man of Sorrows and acquainted with grief. You wept at Lazarus's tomb, and you weep with us. Wrap your tender arms around us and draw us close. Give us the strength to go on and the hope of eternity to sustain us. In the strong name of Jesus I ask, amen.

God Will Never Leave Us

The LORD himself goes before you and will be with you; he will never leave you nor forsake you. Do not be afraid; do not be discouraged.

DEUTERONOMY 31:8

By the time my friend Linda Van Deusen turned nineteen, she'd spent eleven years in hospitals—three of them in a mental hospital.

Her story began with a routine case of chicken pox.

She was three years old when her parents noticed something was dreadfully wrong. The spots had faded, and the itch subsided, but she had begun to limp. Her hands curled under. Her arms became spastic, and her back arched.

We know now she was born with the genetic code for a disease called *dystonia musculorum deformans*. Until she got chicken pox, her immune system had fought dystonia, but when she got sick, her body had to choose whether to fight chicken pox or fight dystonia. It chose chicken pox.

Because dystonia was an unknown disease in the 1950s, rounds of testing revealed nothing. Doctors decided her condition must be an emotional disorder, a ploy to get attention. Every week for several years, her parents drove her fifty miles to Pittsburgh to spend an hour with a psychiatrist. The doctor eventually convinced them he could treat her more effectively if she was hospitalized. Shortly before her eighth birthday, they admitted her to the Children's Hospital in Pittsburgh.

Her case continued to mystify her doctors. We know now that the body uses a chemical called dopamine to help connect the neural pathways in the brain with the neural pathways in the muscles. Her body only produced dopamine while she slept. When the day's supply of dopamine was gone, her body couldn't replenish its supply. Without dopamine, her muscles wouldn't respond.

At breakfast she could feed herself and move almost normally. By lunchtime her body had used up its dopamine, and she couldn't even lift her fork. Gradually she lost her ability to speak above a whisper. Because her ability to perform simple tasks came and went, doctors were convinced her problems were mental, not physical.

"Some days I'd sit with a tray of food in front of me unable to lift my food to my mouth," Linda remembers. "Because the nurses thought I was capable of feeding myself, they wouldn't feed me. Eventually, they'd take the food away. I was a hungry little girl trapped in a body that wouldn't cooperate."[2]

When she turned sixteen, she'd grown too old for the children's hospital, so they transferred her to a mental institution. The next youngest patient was sixty-five years old.

Then her mother had a serious car accident that left her with terrible headaches. When she consulted a neurologist, he suggested surgery, but she declined.

"I have a seriously ill daughter who's not doing well," she said. She showed him the picture of Linda she always carried in her purse. He looked at it for a long time.

"Bring her here," he said. "I want to see her." He'd read about a case of dystonia in medical school and wondered if her symptoms might be coming from this disease.

Five months later, he admitted Linda, now eighteen, to Johns Hopkins Hospital as a research patient. Within two days, they had an accurate diagnosis.

Doctors prescribed a medication called L-dopa. Almost immediately she could brush her teeth, open a carton of milk, and dress herself, actions she'd lost the ability to do. Gradually she learned to walk and talk again.

But her battle wasn't over. Doctors knew the level of medication she took was too high to maintain. Eventually it would stop working. They gave her two options—stay on medication and gradually lose the abilities she'd gained or undergo two life-threatening brain surgeries that would enable her to function on much less medication.

"There's an eighty percent chance you'll die on the operating table," one doctor said.

"What frightened me most wasn't the surgery," Linda remembers, "but the fact that I'd have to stop taking the medication that had restored my ability to move, and, especially, to feed myself. I was so afraid nobody would feed me."

She shared her concerns with her doctor. He looked her in the eye, took her cold hand in his warm one, and said, "Linda, I will come and feed you every meal. I will not let you be hungry."

And he did.

Three meals a day until the day of her surgery.

Linda's doctor promised he wouldn't abandon her. His word gave her the confidence she needed to trust him for whatever lay ahead. He gave her hope for her future.

As God's children, we, too, can have hope—not because of a doctor's (or a spouse's, friend's, or employer's) word. Because our Father, who cannot lie, promised never to leave us nor forsake us.

"The LORD himself goes before you and will be with you; he will never leave you nor forsake you. Do not be afraid; do not be discouraged," He declared in Deuteronomy 31:8.

The word *never* in the original Hebrew is in the absolute negative. In today's vernacular, we'd translate it: "He will never never never never never never leave you nor forsake you." Now that's a promise.

David the psalmist knew the strength of this promise and owned it. "Even though I walk through the darkest valley," he wrote in Psalm 23:4, "I will fear no evil, for *you are with me*" (emphasis added).

Linda's first surgery accomplished nothing. But one month later, after the second surgery, she could talk, move her arms and legs, and feed herself. She still revels in the glorious feeling of squeezing toothpaste onto her brush and brushing her own teeth. Eleven years after they wheeled her into the first hospital, she walked out of one under her own power.

Most of us have never endured an ordeal like Linda's, but some have. A life-altering medical diagnosis, a divorce, a season of infertility, or a difficult ministry position can stretch us to our limits and cause us to doubt our ability to go on.

But when we rest in the promise that God will never never never never never never leave us, we can have hope.

Take Heart

We can trust God for whatever lies ahead. He won't abandon us.

From the Heart

Father, thank you for your promise that you'll never leave me nor forsake me. Others have, and they've broken my heart, but you never will. The Bible reminds me of your faithfulness to believers down through the ages. You didn't abandon them, and you won't abandon me. Because you never change, I can rest in this. Lord, you know the situation that keeps me awake at night and makes me afraid. I'm so grateful I don't have to face it alone. Fill me with the courage that comes from knowing you will never abandon me. Amen.

47

We Will Reap a Harvest

**Let us not become weary in doing good, for
at the proper time we will reap a harvest if
we do not give up.**

GALATIANS 6:9

Trish came to faith in Christ as a twenty-one-year-old college student. One of six sisters, she couldn't wait to share her faith with her family when she returned home on Christmas break. Instead of rejoicing with her, her sisters mocked her faith, calling her "the little church girl." Her parents listened to her animated description of her salvation experience with skepticism and concern, wondering what sort of "cult" she'd been sucked into.

For thirty years Trish has continued to love, serve, and plant spiritual seeds in her family, but they seem as uninterested as they've always been. As her parents draw closer to the end of their lives, Trish often feels discouraged. *What am I doing wrong?* she wonders. *Why doesn't God save them? Why bother trying anymore?*

Maria teaches the Sunday school class no one wants—middle school boys. She spends hours each week preparing lessons she hopes will inspire them. Between addressing behavioral issues and breaking up squabbles, though, she finds little time left to teach. *Am I wasting my time?* she wonders. *Is anything sinking in?* On particularly bad weeks, she mentally composes her resignation letter during the church service, but every Monday morning she opens her teachers guide and begins preparing again.

Shelby is "unequally yoked" to a man who's respectful of her faith but disinterested. In the forty years of their marriage, she's shared the plan of salvation numerous times; coaxed him to attend Christian movies, concerts, and evangelistic events; and prayed thousands of prayers on his behalf. Although she's led dozens of women to faith in Christ through her writing and speaking, she feels like a failure. *If I can't win my husband to Christ,* she thinks, *what right do I have to minister to others?*

Galatians 6:9 provides a fresh infusion of hope to these women and thousands like them who feel weary as they serve God and others.

"Let us not become weary in doing good, for at the proper time we will reap a harvest if we do not give up."

Paul wrote to the church at Galatia. The fledgling church was wrestling through doctrinal challenges, sin issues, and heresy. He ended his fiery letter with words of encouragement and reminded them that God, the Lord of the spiritual harvest, would reward their efforts.

He sets the stage for his words of encouragement by revisiting the laws of sowing and reaping. "Do not be deceived," he assures the believers, "God cannot be mocked. A man reaps what he sows. Whoever sows to please their flesh, from the flesh will reap destruction; whoever sows to please the Spirit, from the Spirit will reap eternal life" (Galatians 6:7–8).

In a garden, we reap what we sow. If we plant beans, beans grow from the soil. If we tuck zucchini seeds into the dirt, zucchini plants will appear, bloom, and produce hundreds and hundreds of pounds of zucchini. Ask me. I did it one year.

In the same way, if I sow the seeds of the flesh—and Paul lists them in Galatians 5—I'll reap the natural outcome of those seeds. Listen to the nasty crop he describes in Galatians 5:19–21: "sexual immorality, impurity and debauchery; idolatry and witchcraft; hatred, discord, jealousy, fits of rage, selfish ambition, dissensions, factions and envy; drunkenness, orgies." Yikes!

But Trish, Maria, and Shelby aren't sowing these seeds. Lord willing, we're not either. As we seek to serve our families, communities, and God, we sow good seeds—"love, joy, peace, forbearance, kindness, goodness, faithfulness, gentleness and self-control" (vv. 22–23).

When we plant these seeds into the lives of those around us, we can rest in the hope that we will reap a harvest if we don't give up. Not might. Not maybe. Not, if we do everything perfectly and never make a mistake. If we stay faithful to the call of God on our lives, we *will* reap a harvest.

There's only one reason our spiritual harvest will fail—if we give up.

Good King Asa ruled over the nation of Judah, sowing spiritual seeds into his nation. He removed foreign altars and Asherah poles. He fortified cities. He called the nation to spiritual revival. For ten years, peace reigned because he set his heart to seek the Lord.

Then trouble came. A Cushite army of "thousands upon thousands" advanced against them. With the Lord's help, Asa and the army of Judah prevailed, but Asa needed encouragement in the wake of such a challenge. God sent a man named Azariah to speak truth into his faltering heart.

"Be strong and *do not give up*, for your work *will* be rewarded" (2 Chronicles 15:7, emphasis added).

We find it easy to love, serve, and witness to those around us when the world is peaceful, and we see the rewards for our efforts. But when we have to go to battle, we often grow weary. We lose hope and want to quit.

If we quit, we fail. If we press on, God promises, we'll reap a harvest.

I don't know about you, but I want to reap a rich spiritual harvest. More than I want to harvest hundreds of pounds of zucchini, I want to see hundreds of souls in heaven—especially those I love—because I didn't quit.

And so we press on in hope, knowing we *will* reap a harvest.

Take Heart

If I don't give up, I will reap a glorious harvest that will last for all eternity.

From the Heart

Lord, I'm so grateful you set in place the laws of sowing and reaping. Thank you for the sure and certain hope that you'll reward my efforts to sow spiritual seeds and bring about an eternal harvest. I confess that I grow weary in doing good. I lose sight of your promise when I can't see results right now. Grow my faith. Infuse my tired faith with new passion. Enable me to press on. Help me walk in the strength only you can provide. In Jesus's name I ask, amen.

48

While There Is Breath, There Is Hope

**Anyone who is among
the living has hope.**

ECCLESIASTES 9:4

I'd never seen someone as sick as James. Ravaged by a disease for which there was no cure, he lay in a physician-induced coma at a local hospital. HIV had stolen his well-padded frame, leaving a skeleton in its place. Sharp angles and prominent bones lay under the skin that stretched tightly across his face. The respirator taped to his mouth hissed like an asthmatic, forcing air into lungs unable to rise on their own.

"If his organs begin to shut down," the attending physician said, "it's only a matter of time."

James's family kept vigil by his bedside, and a steady stream of friends stopped by the hospital. They tiptoed into the sterile room, squeezed James's hand, and left, smothering tears as they turned away.

"He's so young," James's mother wept into her hands. "He hasn't even finished college. Or found a real job. Or gotten married."

Many of us who had known him from youth group fasted and prayed. One night, leaving his room after another heartbreaking visit, I encountered our pastor.

"I'm so afraid for James," I confessed. "I don't know if he can ever recover."

Pastor John nodded, acknowledging the legitimacy of my concern. "He is a very sick young man."

He met my eyes, then looked beyond me to a window overlooking the city. In the distance, a church steeple rose, its white spire pointing toward heaven. A cross perched atop the structure glistened against the evening sky.

He straightened his shoulders, inhaled deeply, and turned to me.

"But while there is breath, there is hope."

He reached for the door handle and slipped into the room, leaving me to ponder his words.

King Solomon, the wisest man who ever lived, wrote about end-of-life issues in the short Old Testament book of Ecclesiastes. Considered by many to be the reflections of a jaded, disillusioned man, the book contains the declaration, "The living know that they will die" (Ecclesiastes 9:5).

Set alongside this sobering reality, though, is the same uplifting, prayer-energizing perspective my pastor shared, "Anyone who is among the living has hope" (v. 4).

As I left the hospital that night, Pastor John's words floated toward me like a life ring. They challenged my fear that there was no hope of recovery for James. That the seriousness of his illness and the statistics his doctors had quoted had the final say. That prayer wouldn't change anything.

I shared Pastor John's words with my husband. "While there is breath, there is hope." I shared them with James's friends from youth group. I shared them with his mother the next day when I visited.

"Don't give up. Don't stop praying. While there is breath, there's hope."

We renewed our determination to pray. Church members posted the need on church prayer chains and prayed by his bedside. Hope infused our thinking and drove us to our knees over and over again.

His nurse was elated when James's oxygen stats began to improve. Then his kidney output increased. His heart rate, which had been weak and sluggish, strengthened. Every day he made progress.

Gradually they dialed back the medicine that sedated him and weaned him from the respirator.

I don't know if my change in perspective impacted James's condition, but I do know God moves His people to pray when He wants to work in someone's life. In His mercy, God had determined to restore James to health. Two months after the ambulance delivered him to the emergency room, his mother wheeled him through the door of his home to the cheers of family and friends.

"Now that's a sight I wasn't sure we'd see," Pastor John said, wiping the corners of his eyes.

"I didn't either," I said, "but you were right. While there is breath, there is hope."

I know God doesn't choose to heal everyone. Tiny children struggle with cancer. Teenagers die in car wrecks. The elderly wrestle through the ravages of age-related illness. Eventually, death comes to all of us.

But only God decides when each of us will die. "All the days ordained for me were written in your book before one of them came to be," the psalmist declared (Psalm 139:16). Until He shows us otherwise, He calls us to pray. Oftentimes, He uses the prayers of His people to bring about the healing He ordains.

If you're praying for a sick loved one today, don't stop. Remember Solomon's wise observation, "Anyone who is among the living has hope."

Take Heart

Only God, not doctors, nurses, or statistics, decides the length of a person's life. While there is breath, there is hope.

From the Heart

Father, thank you for reminding us through your Word that you order and direct our days. May I never cease to pray for someone because "the odds aren't good" or the illness seems too severe. You are the God of miracles. Nothing is too hard for you. Strengthen my faith and help me pray for your will to be done on Earth as it is in heaven, amen.

49

Every Gift Matters

**God has placed the parts in the body, every
one of them, just as he wanted them to be.**

1 CORINTHIANS 12:18

My friend Jean is a skilled writer with a brilliant theological mind.
When the website she writes for handed out assignments, she chose
the topic of soteriology. The next week she chose Pelagianism.

Huh? What?

When she told me, I had to ask Google how to spell the terms and
then define them. But Jean wrote two thousand words on each of
these doctrines. Weeks later, she can still hold an articulate conversation on their origin, growth, and theological ramifications.

While I find these subjects slightly interesting in a church-history-
and-theology kind of way, I couldn't write two hundred words, let
alone two thousand, on either one. And weeks later, if you asked me
to explain them, despite Jean's skillful writing, I'd be like the kid
who read the CliffsNotes on *Moby Dick* the night before the test. Uh,

whale? Yes! There *was* a whale. And a fisherman—in a boat. With a harpoon . . . I think.

Then there's my friend Cam. She researched her family tree for almost a decade and traced her ancestors all the way back to colonial days. And when she found a branch that led to William Molineux, one of the signers of the Declaration of Independence? The discovery sparked a writing project that produced a three-hundred-page historically accurate novel about the American Revolution. It took her *ten years* to write and research it. It doesn't just contain historically accurate dates and events—every scene is filled with settings, language, and people exactly as they happened almost three hundred years ago.

When I compare my writing to Jean's or Cam's, if my perspective isn't right, I feel like a kindergartener among graduating seniors. They write theological and historical tomes, and I write eight-hundred-word devotions. They handle complex concepts, and I specialize in simple. They use multisyllabic words like Pelagianism and soteriology, and I focus on words like hope and faith.

You might not be a writer, but I suspect you've compared your gifts and abilities to someone else's and come up lacking. Especially at church.

Robin can play the piano *and* sing, but you can barely hold a hymnal without dropping it. And carry a tune? Uh, no. Please, go sing on a hill far away—far, far away.

Sarah can teach—oh, my, can she teach. When she opens her mouth the most engaging questions flow off her tongue, sparking animated discussion and expansive learning. You, in comparison, can't even get the first graders in your class to say their memory verses unless you bribe them with candy.

Perhaps this is why the apostle Paul devoted three chapters of the book of 1 Corinthians to the subject of spiritual gifts—to give us hope. If the Corinthian church was anything like our churches, it was filled with members devaluing their gifts and coveting everyone else's. Like kids eyeing other kids' candy haul on Halloween, believers often fail to embrace their own spiritual gifts and long for what someone else has.

Paul, writing under the inspiration of the Holy Spirit, determined to set them straight. In his discourse, we learn much about our giftedness and find solid reasons to hope in our unique equipping. Listen to his words:

> There are different kinds of gifts, but the same Spirit distributes them. There are different kinds of service, but the same Lord. There are different kinds of working, but in all of them and in everyone it is the same God at work.
>
> Now to each one the manifestation of the Spirit is given for the common good. . . . All these are the work of one and the same Spirit, and he distributes them to each one, just as he determines. (1 Corinthians 12:4–7, 11)

When I feel hopeless and useless as I compare my writing abilities to my friends' or my spiritual gifts to other Christians', God's words to me through Paul envelope me in a holy hug: "God has placed the parts in the body, every one of them, just as he wanted them to be" (v. 18).

Just as He wanted them to be.

Praise Jesus, He doesn't want me to write articles on soteriology or Pelagianism. Nor does He intend for me to write a 300-page historical novel. He's given me the gift of devotion writing and will use me and my words exactly how He wants to.

Maybe God has gifted you to sing, play the piano, or teach, or perhaps He's given you a different gift. Maybe He's filled you with the gift of helps so you can come alongside those who need assistance. Or He's given you the gift of discernment so you can lend wise counsel to those who are confused. Or the gift of compassion so you can comfort crying babies in the nursery so their weary parents can attend church undistracted.

Whatever gift God has given us, we can rest in hope and confidence, because we know God gifted us and placed us in the body of Christ just as He wanted us to be.

"Now you are the body of Christ, and each one of you is a part of it" (v. 27). May we glorify God by using our gifts together.

Take Heart

Because God has gifted and placed each of us in the body of Christ just as He wanted us to be, we can exercise our gifts in confident hope that He will use them for His glory.

From the Heart

Lord, everywhere I look I see gifted people doing great things for you. And then I look at myself. Some days it's hard not to envy their talents or disparage my own. Thank you for reminding me that you've given each of us the exact gifts needed to accomplish our part in your good work. Enable me to accomplish everything you've ordained for me to do, big or small, for your glory.

50

Share the Reason for Your Hope

**Always be prepared to give an
answer to everyone who asks you to give
the reason for the hope that you have.
But do this with gentleness and respect.**

1 PETER 3:15

Ibanez and Consuela were as broken a couple as I've ever seen. They sat on the sofa as far away from each other as they could possibly sit. He stared at his feet, refusing to make eye contact as we introduced ourselves. She met our gaze, but tears formed in the corners of her brown eyes, threatening to spill over if she blinked.

My husband, David, and I were three days into a ten-day mission trip. Our missionary friends had persuaded us to offer marriage and family counseling to couples associated with their church. Although we'd agreed to help with everything they'd asked us to do, we balked at their request to offer counseling.

"We're not professionally trained," we protested. "What could we offer them?"

"You may not be trained," our missionary friend Guillermo said, "but you've walked with the Lord for many years and led marriage and family Bible studies. You know more biblical truth than these couples do. It would mean a lot to us—and to them."

We reluctantly agreed, and when counseling day came, our hearts trembled. What in the world could we say? *Lord*, we prayed as the first couple walked into our hotel sitting room, *please give us the words.*

I don't know who was more uncomfortable, us or them, but I remember there was a lot of feet shuffling and throat clearing before Guillermo, serving as our translator, opened the session with prayer.

"Ibanez and Consuela," he said, "what brings you here today?"

Ibanez stared at the floor while Consuela told their story. She spoke slowly, reluctant to acknowledge the path they'd traveled but desperate to find a way forward. A series of shady business dealings had bankrupted their family business. When creditors threatened to take their home, Consuela went back to work, leaving their twin daughters with a sitter. Instead of seeking employment, Ibanez sought solace at the neighborhood bar—where he met a woman. Soon he had added infidelity to the list of strikes against their marriage, leaving their lives broken and hopeless.

Every sentence from Consuela's mouth disclosed another bad choice, but I didn't want her to stop talking. I knew when she finished, she'd expect us to say something helpful, wise, and life changing.

Oh, Lord, I prayed silently, *this situation is broken in so many ways. There's no way it can be fixed. Where do we even begin? Without a miracle, this couple has no hope.*

Through the fog of my prayers, I heard David speaking and Guillermo translating.

"Your relationship is badly damaged." Ibanez squirmed, and Consuela nodded. A tear escaped from her eye. "Jesus is your only hope. If you confess your sins and surrender your lives to Him, He'll forgive you."

David laid his hand on his chest and patted it. "He'll come and live inside your heart and change you. I know He can do this because He did it for me. And for my wife. And for Guillermo."

"I was a teenage alcoholic and a drug user," he said. For the first time Ibanez raised his head. "I didn't care about anything except the next high. But when I asked Christ to be my Savior, He came to live within me. Little by little, He changed me. He'll change you, too, if you let Him."

As Guillermo translated, David explained the gospel in clear and simple terms. He ended by asking, "Would you like to ask Christ to be your Savior?"

A light came into Ibanez's eyes—a hungry light. A hopeful light. He reached across the sofa and clasped his wife's hand.

"Sí." He nodded, and she did, too.

"Sí."

While Guillermo led them in prayer, I prayed, too. *I'm so sorry, Lord. I forgot your command in 1 Peter 3:15: "Always be prepared to give an answer to everyone who asks you to give the reason for the hope that you have." Jesus is the answer to every problem we face, no matter how bad it seems. Forgive me for thinking any situation or any person is so broken that Jesus can't fix them.*

When I opened my eyes, I saw Ibanez sitting with his arm around Consuela's shoulders. Both were smiling broadly. I smiled too. In my best preschool Spanish, I said, *"Eres mi hermano y hermana en Cristo."* You are my brother and sister in Christ.

Life didn't change immediately for Ibanez and Consuela, but little by little God transformed their lives and healed their relationship. When we returned to the church years later, Ibanez was the first to greet us. "I want to thank you for all you did for my wife and me," he said, grasping David's hand and pumping it hard. "We are very grateful."

I'm grateful, too. David's faithfulness to share the gospel with Ibanez and Consuela and their eagerness to accept it reminded me I should always be prepared to share the reason for the hope I have—and this hope is Jesus.

Take Heart

Jesus calls those of us who hope in Christ to be prepared to share our hope with others—with gentleness and respect.

From the Heart

Lord, I confess. Sometimes I look at the broken lives around me and wonder if some are beyond hope. Yet I know better. I've seen what you've done in my life and in the lives of others. You bring beauty from ashes and transform every lost soul who puts their trust in you. Give me eyes to see where you're at work in the world and courage to share the reason for my hope. Help me point people to you and trust you to change their lives.

51

You Still Have Work to Do

**I am torn between the two: I desire
to depart and be with Christ, which is
better by far; but it is more necessary
for you that I remain in the body.**

PHILIPPIANS 1:23-24

"I don't know why God hasn't taken me home yet," Betty said. "So many of my friends have already gone on to be with the Lord."

We were visiting together in the assisted living center where Betty had lived since her husband died seven years earlier.

"I've lived a full life," she said. "I'm at peace with God, and I'm ready to go." She threaded her arthritis-twisted fingers together and sighed. "And besides that, I'm tired."

We talked a bit more, and our conversation turned, as it always did, to our families.

"Lillian made a profession of faith last week, and I got to see her baptized," she said with a smile. "I'm worried about John, though. He's not very interested in spiritual things." She lifted her cataract-clouded eyes to meet mine, and her eyebrows pinched together. "I pray for him every day. Some days, when I can get these clumsy old fingers to work right, I text him Bible verses. I remind him that I love him, and God loves him."

A resident walked past her open door pushing a walker.

"Hey, Mary," Betty said with a wave. She waited until the woman had shuffled down the hall before she spoke again. "Mary's my next-door neighbor. When she first moved in, she wouldn't talk to anyone and had all her meals brought to her room. I knocked on her door one day and introduced myself. Found out she has no family and no friends." A mischievous smile crinkled Betty's face. "I decided I'd be her friend whether she liked it or not."

"Good for you," I said, returning her grin. "How's that working out?"

"Well, I still don't think she's crazy about me, but she has a sweet tooth, and she likes the cookies my daughter brings. We're getting together for a cup of decaf tomorrow. I'm going to share my copy of the *Our Daily Bread* devotional with her."

As I walked to the parking lot after our visit, I thought about Betty's words. "I know why God hasn't taken you home yet, Betty," I said to no one in particular. "He still has work for you to do."

The apostle Paul could identify with Betty. He wasn't eighty-five years old and living in an assisted living center, but he felt the weariness of his life on Earth and the tug of heaven.

"I am torn between the two," he wrote to the Philippians. "I desire to depart and be with Christ, which is better by far; but it is more necessary for you that I remain in the body" (Philippians 1:23–24).

Struggling under physical weakness, suffering persecution for his faith, and bearing the daily burdens of the churches under his care, he longed to be released from his mortality and join his Savior in heaven. Yet he knew God had extended his life for good reasons.

The church needed him. The disciples needed him. The kingdom needed him. "It is more necessary for you that I remain in the body," he told the Philippian church (v. 24). He knew he still had work to do and souls to reach. "If I am to go on living in the body, this will mean fruitful labor for me" (v. 22).

Although he yearned for heaven, he surrendered the length of his life and the timing of his death to God. He determined to remain faithful to God and serve Him in whatever capacity He granted him, no matter how difficult his remaining years became. "I eagerly expect and hope that I will in no way be ashamed, but will have sufficient courage so that now as always Christ will be exalted in my body, whether by life or by death. For to me, to live is Christ and to die is gain" (vv. 20–21).

Why did the apostle Paul and Betty live as long as they did? Because they still had work to do.

And so do we.

Regardless of whether we die robust and in full command of our minds and bodies or frail and struggling to take our last breath, we can rest in hope that God has a purpose for every day of our lives. As we walk in faith and surrender ourselves to His care, we can rest in God's sovereignty. We need never doubt the reason for our existence nor fear our latter days. God holds our lives in His hand.

Take Heart

The truth that God has a purpose for every day of our lives enables us to live out our days in hope.

From the Heart

Father, some days I doubt the reason for my existence. When I feel useless, remind me that all the days ordained for me were written in your book before one of them came to be (Psalm 139:16). Not one of them is a mistake. Because you created me to do good works, help me live each day on mission. Show me ways to minister to others, despite my limitations, and point people to you. In the name of the Lord Jesus Christ I ask, amen.

52

God's Word Helps Us Battle the Enemy

I rise before dawn and cry for help;
I have put my hope in your word.

PSALM 119:147

The chant began slowly, but grew in volume, tempo, and intensity until it filled the stadium. Fifty thousand men, part of a team united in purpose and vision, had gathered in Folsom Field in Boulder, Colorado, for the biggest coaching event of the year. Reverend E.V. Hill, a pastor from Los Angeles, shared a strategy from the master playbook.

"Hit 'em. Hit 'em! *Hit 'em!*"[3]

As he described the ultimate play in the battle against the enemy of our souls, the stadium was practically silent. Men leaned forward in their seats, eager to hear the secret to victory over Satan and his schemes.

Dr. Hill stepped closer to the microphone and paused, seeming to make eye contact with every man in the crowd. "Jesus said, 'Devil, it is written.'

"He went to the book of Deuteronomy and came out with Scripture. Every time the devil opened his mouth, Jesus threw Scripture in it. He said, 'Devil, it is written, "Man shall not live by bread alone." It is written, "Thou shalt not tempt the Lord thy God."' He hit him over and over and over with the Scripture.

"And guess what happened?" he asked the spellbound crowd. "The devil *ran*."

The men erupted in cheers, pumped their fists, and raised their arms in celebration.

"You don't have to take it. You don't have to take the devil's mess. You don't have to take his stuff. Hit 'em with the Word. Take out your Bible and hit. That. Devil. With the Word."

Buoyed by the truth of Scripture and the power of the Holy Spirit, the stadium echoed Dr. Hill's words in a battle cry.

"Hit 'em. Hit 'em! Hit 'em!"

I didn't attend the Promise Keepers conference in 1993, but I've probably watched the YouTube video of Dr. Hill's message fifty times. When I grow discouraged and wonder if I'll ever win my battle with the world, the flesh, and the devil, it reminds me that God's Word is powerful.

The psalmist knew this. In one of the most beautiful tributes to the Word of God, Psalm 119, he wrote, "I rise before dawn and cry for help; I have put my hope in your word. My eyes stay open through the watches of the night, that I may meditate on your promises" (Psalm 119:147–148).

As the psalmist did, I've often laid awake nights fretting and fearful. My mind swirls with faithless thoughts and churns with real or imagined trouble. *What will I do if something happens to my husband? Will my children and grandchildren love God? Will the money we've saved carry us through retirement? Will I or someone I love die of some terrible disease?*

Then the voice of the enemy adds his running commentary. *How can you call yourself a Christian when you still struggle with ____? Why do you keep praying for them? Nothing ever changes.*

Then God, through the Bible verses I've memorized, whispers truth to my troubled soul.

"Never will I leave you; never will I forsake you" (Hebrews 13:5).

"The prayer of a righteous person is powerful and effective" (James 5:16).

"And my God will meet all your needs according to the riches of his glory in Christ Jesus" (Philippians 4:19).

My fears (and Satan's lies) scuttle off into the shadows as I shine the light of God's Word. I cling to His promises like a hiker clutching a flashlight as he searches for the way out of an inky black cave.

"Therefore, there is now no condemnation for those who are in Christ Jesus" (Romans 8:1).

"The eyes of the LORD are on the righteous, and his ears are attentive to their cry" (Psalm 34:15).

"Let us not become weary in doing good, for at the proper time we will reap a harvest if we do not give up" (Galatians 6:9).

Like Jesus in the desert, the psalmist in Israel, and E.V. Hill in Folsom Field, I raise the weapon of God's Word in faith. Every time I do, God equips me to rest in peace and hope. Armed with Scripture to meet my every need, I find strength to walk in victory and rest in peace.

Take Heart

Because God's Word is true, we can find courage and hope to defeat all our fears.

From the Heart

Father, I pray with the psalmist, "Hear my voice in accordance with your love; preserve my life, O LORD, according to your laws" (Psalm 119:149). Thank you for giving me the powerful weapon of your Word. Remind me, every day, that I need not be the victim of Satan's lies or my own fears. Help me walk in hope, knowing that the truth of Scripture will always prevail. In the strong name of Jesus I ask, amen.

53

God Offers Hope through Repentance

We have been unfaithful to our God by marrying foreign women from the peoples around us. But in spite of this, there is still hope for Israel.

EZRA 10:2

Liza buried her head in the crook of her arm and sobbed. Great, gut-wrenching sobs shook her shoulders and took her breath away. When she asked to meet with me, I knew something serious was going on, but I wasn't prepared for this.

I'd known Liza since she was a toddler in the church nursery. The awkwardness of adolescence had transformed the carefree, golden-haired child into a quiet, serious teenager, but she faithfully attended the youth events we hosted at our home. In her senior year, she volunteered to serve in our youth group and mentored a cluster of middle school girls.

She was accepted at the local university, and I assumed she'd continue to attend our church, but her attendance became sporadic. Her mother's prayer requests added to my fears that Liza had wandered away from the Lord.

Liza's phone call that one winter morning caught me by surprise.

"May I come over?" she said. "I need someone to talk to."

I figured she'd share boy troubles or class struggles, but I was unprepared for the flood of emotion that erupted from her.

"I got arrested last night," she said, barely able to squeeze out the words. "For the second time. DUI."

I handed her a tissue, and she pressed it against her eyelids, leaving black mascara smudges around her eyes.

"I started drinking at parties. Just to fit in. But it got out of control. I'm having trouble making it to class. I'm failing chemistry. And now I might lose my driver's license."

She raised her eyes, blurry with tears and regret.

"I know I deserve whatever punishment I get."

Lowering her head, she said in a voice thick with emotion, "I'm so ashamed. I've disappointed my parents. I've let my family down." She took a great, hiccupy breath and let it out in a sigh. "Worst of all," she whispered, "I've sinned against God."

I suspect the men of Ezra's day felt somewhat like Liza. These men were the first of their generation to set foot in the holy city after Cyrus, king of the Babylonian Empire, allowed the exiles to return to Jerusalem. The men had begun well. They started rebuilding the temple and restoring their city. It wasn't long, however, until they departed from God's principles, became saturated by the culture of the surrounding nations, and married pagan women.

When Ezra the priest arrived, the leaders came to him with their confession.

"The people of Israel, including the priests and the Levites, have not kept themselves separate from the neighboring peoples with their detestable practices. . . . They have taken some of their daughters as wives for themselves and their sons, and have mingled the holy race with the peoples around them. And the leaders and officials have led the way in this unfaithfulness" (Ezra 9:1–2).

Overwhelmed by the depth of the Israelites' sin, Ezra tore his robe, pulled hair from his head and beard, and sat, appalled, until the time of the evening sacrifice. Then he fell on his knees, raised his hands toward heaven, and prayed, "I am too ashamed and disgraced, my God, to lift up my face to you, because our sins are higher than our heads and our guilt has reached to the heavens" (v. 6).

The men, women, and children of the town gathered around him, devastated by the depth of their sin. Weeping bitterly, they repented and confessed.

"We have been unfaithful to our God by marrying foreign women from the peoples around us," one person cried on behalf of the people. "But in spite of this, there is still hope for Israel" (10:2).

In spite of this, there is still hope.

I shared their words with Liza, and a glint of light shone in her tearful eyes.

"'If we confess our sins,' 1 John 1:9 promises, 'he is faithful and just and will forgive us our sins and purify us from all unrighteousness,'" I said. "You need to confess your sin to God first. Tell Him everything you've done. He knows it anyway, but you need to confess it for your benefit. Then receive the forgiveness He offers."

She nodded, bowed her head, and prayed the most repentant, tender prayer of confession I've ever heard.

"Now go talk to your parents," I said. "Tell them the same things you told me and ask for their forgiveness. They're going to be hurt and upset, but they love you. They'll help you through this." I wrapped my arms around her and squeezed tightly.

"It's going to take time to restore what you've lost, and there are going to be consequences. But God specializes in taking broken things and making them whole again. In spite of this, there is still hope."

Liza's journey back to spiritual and physical health wasn't an easy journey. Neither was the Israelites'. They had to take painful steps to separate themselves from the sin they'd chosen to engage in. But in time, God brought healing.

Four years after Eliza's tearful confession, she walked across the stage to accept her degree in early childhood education. The only smiles bigger than hers were the ones that shone on her parents' faces. And (I suspect) the Lord's.

Take Heart

No matter what we've done, God will always hear our sincere prayer of repentance and extend His forgiveness.

From the Heart

Father, like the men of Israel during the time of Ezra, I don't always walk in your ways. Sometimes, even though I know what your will is, I do the opposite. I want my own way and care little about offending you. Forgive me for the sins of independence, pride, and disobedience. Cleanse my heart. Restore my fellowship with you. Help me walk in your ways all the days of my life. In the kind and merciful name of Jesus I ask, amen.

54

Our Families Don't Disqualify Us

For the director of music.
A *maskil* of the Sons of Korah.

PSALM 42

"My grandfather was an alcoholic. My father was an alcoholic. By the time I was seventeen years old, I was an alcoholic." My husband, David, shares his story whenever he gets a chance. One day he spoke to the youth group at our church. "Dad was a mean drunk. He was verbally and physically abusive. Eventually, his drinking destroyed his marriage and ruined our family."

"The saddest part of all," David said, "is that I became just like him. Even though I saw what alcohol did to his life, I followed in his footsteps. By the time I was a junior in high school, I lived from one drink to the next. I used drugs, too. I was always looking for the next high. Always trying to numb the pain."

"When I became a Christian," he continued, making eye contact with each of the four boys slouched on the back row, "I wondered if I'd be able to break free from the chains that held me and so many of my family members. What made me think I could break the cycle?"

He took a deep breath, lost in the memory. "Even after God took alcohol and drugs out of my life, I wondered if my past disqualified me to do anything for Him. Maybe my family was too disgraceful for God to use me."

I wonder if the descendants of Korah wondered the same thing.

You may remember that Korah, along with Datham and Abiram, "became insolent and rose up against Moses. With them were 250 Israelite men, well-known community leaders who had been appointed members of the council" (Numbers 16:1–2). They challenged the priestly roles of Moses and Aaron and attempted to overthrow their leadership. Moses responded by inviting God to settle the dispute.

"If the Lord brings about something totally new," Moses said, "and the earth opens its mouth and swallows them, with everything that belongs to them, and they go down alive into the realm of the dead, then you will know that these men have treated the Lord with contempt" (v. 30).

God's response was swift and earth-shattering: "As soon as he finished saying all this, the ground under them split apart and the earth opened its mouth and swallowed them and their households, and all those associated with Korah, together with their possessions. They went down alive into the realm of the dead, with everything they owned; the earth closed over them, and they perished and were gone from the community" (vv. 31–33).

Korah's sons, perhaps too young (or maybe too wise) to be associated with their father's rebellion, were spared (Numbers 26:11).

Imagine what it was like to walk through the Israelite camp after God had judged their father.

"Yep, he's one of those Korahites," a neighbor might mutter. "They deserved everything they got."

"Can you believe the audacity of that man? Thinking he could challenge Moses . . . "

"The family's homeless, you know. Everything they owned got swallowed up with him."

Yet God was merciful. He didn't punish the sons for the sins of their father (Deuteronomy 24:16). Korah's line wasn't extinguished, nor were they disqualified from serving God. Generations later, Samuel, the prophet and judge, a descendant of Korah, served as priest before the Lord (1 Chronicles 6:31–38; 1 Samuel 1:1). The Korahites became doorkeepers and custodians for the tabernacle (1 Chronicles 9:19–21). One group of Korahites joined King David's army and became expert warriors (12:6).

In a serendipitous twist, the descendants of Korah became musicians in residence in the tabernacle during the time of King David. They played, sang, and composed music for the pageantry associated with the ark of the covenant's return to Jerusalem. Eleven psalms in the Bible (42, 44–49, 84–85, and 87–88) are credited to "the sons of Korah."

One of their most well-known psalms describes an earthquake: "God is our refuge and strength. . . . Therefore we will not fear, though the earth give way and the mountains fall into the heart of the sea, though its waters roar and foam and the mountains quake with their surging" (Psalm 46:1–3). What powerful imagery!

One wonders if the poet who penned [the lyrics of Psalm 46] was remembering his ignoble beginnings, his distant ancestor who perished in an earthquake for his pride and rebellion. Perhaps it was that reflection that prompted the following words of the same psalm: "He says, 'Be still, and know that I am God; I will be exalted among the nations, I will be exalted in the earth'" (Psalm 46:10).[4]

The sons of Korah provide biblical proof and hope that God doesn't hold us accountable for our parents', grandparents', or other ancestors' sinful choices. Nor are we doomed to repeat them.

"Therefore," the apostle Paul declared to the believers in Corinth, former pagans who'd been delivered from gross immorality and sexual sin, "if anyone is in Christ, the new creation has come: The old has gone, the new is here!" (2 Corinthians 5:17).

My husband, David, concluded his youth group talk with these words, "No matter what you or your family members have done, God will forgive you. He'll cleanse your hearts, transform your lives, and use you in His service. My parents didn't walk with God until later in life, but God didn't disqualify me because of them. He saved me, called me into the ministry, and continues to use me to share the gospel. He can do the same for you."

When we struggle with hopelessness because of our past or the sins of our family, we sometimes wonder if we're of any use to God. Thankfully the sons of Korah give us hope. They remain a shining example of how God helps people overcome the effects of wicked and dysfunctional families and serve Him with honor and joy.

Take Heart

God never disqualifies us from serving Him because of our family's faithlessness or sin.

From the Heart

Father, I bring no spiritual heritage with me as I seek to follow you. I'm glad you don't require a pedigree or an impeccable family lineage to become part of your work. Thank you for grafting me into a new family—your family. Knowing I'm one of your children gives me hope and joy.

55

Our Faith Is Reasonable

**For we did not follow cleverly devised
stories when we told you about the coming
of our Lord Jesus Christ in power, but we
were eyewitnesses of his majesty.**

2 PETER 1:16

True confession. I struggle with choices.

Many of my friends view choices as an invitation to explore new and glorious options. Thirty choices at their favorite ice-cream store? Bring 'em on! Twenty hotels within a five-mile radius of their vacation spot? Sweet. A thousand books to peruse at the used bookstore? A dream come true.

Me? Choices make me want to cower under my bed. A six-page menu at a restaurant paralyzes me. What if the entree doesn't taste as good as the picture looks? What if I like my old standby better, and I'm disappointed? What if I spend the extra money, and it just doesn't measure up? If a friend invites me to a new restaurant, you'd better believe I'd go online and study the menu in advance. Otherwise, we'd sit there for thirty minutes while I waffle between veggie quiche and grilled pimento cheese.

It's not that I'm afraid to choose. I'm just afraid to choose wrongly. The weight of consequences is real. A poor choice from a restaurant menu isn't a big deal. I can always order something else. But the choices I make that will impact the rest of my life? My family's life? My eternal life? These are weighty.

I often share how, as an eighteen-year-old, I became overwhelmed by the significant life decisions I faced. Who to date and (eventually) marry. Where to go to school. What major to study. The most important choice I made, without realizing its significance, was the decision to place my faith in Jesus Christ.

Uncharacteristically, I did very little research before surrendering my life and my eternity to God. The pastor at the church I'd been attending did it for me. Week after week he shared compelling and convincing verses that resonated within my soul. *This* choice—this glorious, terrifying, supernaturally wonderful offer to forgive my sin, cleanse my soul, and make a new person out of messy me—was too compelling to pass up.

Only later did I learn of historical and scientific reasons to believe the Bible and Jesus's claim that He is *the* way, *the* truth, and *the* life, and that no one comes to the Father but through Him (John 14:6).

I discovered reasonable and reliable evidence abounds to prove His resurrection. Books like *Evidence that Demands a Verdict* and *The Case for Christ* affirmed that Jesus lived, died, and rose again. These works, written by converted skeptics, drew heavily from the Jewish historian Josephus's objective account of the events that occurred around the time of Christ.

I learned that Christ's resurrection is the foundation on which all other doctrines rest. If Jesus didn't rise from the dead, He had no power to raise anyone else from the dead. And He certainly couldn't promise us eternal life. His resurrection not only proved His triumph over death, hell, and the grave; it confirmed God had accepted His sacrificial death on the cross. No other faith has a resurrected Savior.

As I visited creation science websites, I learned of the unshakable scientific and archaeological evidence that supports the validity of the Bible and its account of the history of the world. Biblical cities deemed "mythical" by skeptics came to light as modern archaeologists unearthed ancient city ruins. The Dead Sea Scrolls, discovered by a young Bedouin shepherd in 1947, proved that God had preserved the integrity and accuracy of His Word for millennia.

This evidence didn't cause me to believe. It reinforced what I'd already believed by faith. No amount of evidence will be enough to convince a person to place their faith in Christ. We must always accept certain aspects of the Christian life by faith. "Without faith," Hebrews 11:6 declares, "it is impossible to please God."

I'm glad faith isn't a blind leap in the dark. It isn't believing in something with no reason, evidence, or proof. We don't have to hope we're right. We can know. As the apostle Peter said, "For we did not follow cleverly devised stories when we told you about the coming of our Lord Jesus Christ in power, but we were eyewitnesses of his majesty" (2 Peter 1:16). He and five hundred others testified to what they *saw*.

Biblical faith is reasonable and intelligent. It holds its own against every branch of science. Instead of contradicting science, it reinforces it. As my friend Bob Hostetler says, "Christians don't have to check their brains at the door."

When Jesus walked the earth, He declared He was "*the* way and *the* truth and *the* life." Science, history, and archaeology give us ample reasons to believe Him. This is crucial, because "no one comes to the Father except through [Him]" (John 14:6).

I'm grateful God protected me from false teachers and doctrine in the early years of my life. By His grace, He placed people around me who knew and loved the one true God and shared Him with others. They sowed spiritual seeds that blossomed into a vibrant and hope-filled faith. Based on truth, I have a sure and certain hope that my faith will culminate in eternal life.

Take Heart

A preponderance of the evidence gives us hope to confidently believe Christ's claim that He is *the* way, *the* truth, and *the* life.

From the Heart

Father God, there are so many religions, paths, and spiritual schools of thought. Thank you for protecting me from confusion and reinforcing that what I believe is true. I'm so grateful I can stake my hope firmly on the solid ground of Jesus. Thank you for the trustworthiness of the Bible. Thank you for giving us a solid source of wisdom we can base our lives (and our eternities) on. I love you so much, amen.

56

Standing Strong during Trials

But the Lord stood at my side and gave me strength.

2 TIMOTHY 4:17

Every morning at daybreak for seventeen years, Dmitri would stand at attention by the bed in his prison cell. He'd face the east, raise his arms in praise to God, and sing a heart song to Jesus.

Nik Ripken's book *The Insanity of God: A True Story of Faith Resurrected* describes how other prisoners laughed, cursed, and jeered at him. "They'd bang metal cups against the iron bars in angry protest. They threw food and sometimes human waste to try to shut him up and extinguish the only true light shining in that dark place every morning at dawn."[5]

Dmitri was a Russian pastor sentenced to life imprisonment for leading an unauthorized house church. He didn't set out to become a pastor, but because the nearest church was a three-day walk from his village, he became concerned that his sons were growing up without knowing Scripture. Once a week he'd gather his family, read the Bible, and share the stories he'd learned from his Christian parents.

The village was small, and the walls were thin. Soon neighbors asked to join them. As townspeople heard of the powerful manifestations of God taking place among the worshippers, more and more crowded into Dmitri's home to hear about Jesus. One night, more than one hundred fifty people gathered.

The authorities couldn't let this continue. They arrested Dmitri, sent him a thousand kilometers away, and imprisoned him. He was the only believer among one thousand five hundred hardened criminals. His captors tortured him to force him to renounce his faith, but Dmitri held firm.

One day, Dmitri found a full sheet of paper and a pencil in the prison yard. "I rushed back to my jail cell, and I wrote every Scripture reference, every Bible verse, every story, and every song I could recall."[6] He posted it on a damp pipe in his cell as an offering to the Lord. When his jailor saw it, he beat and punished him and threatened him with execution.

As jailors dragged him from his cell and down the corridor, "the strangest thing happened. Before they reached the door leading to the courtyard—before stepping out into the place of execution—fifteen hundred hardened criminals stood at attention by their beds. They faced the east and they began to sing . . . the heart song they had heard Dmitri sing to Jesus every morning for all those years."[7]

Shocked, his jailors released their hold and backed away from him.

"Who are you?" one demanded. Dmitri straightened and stood as tall and as proudly as he could.

"I am a son of the Living God, and Jesus is His name!" The guards returned him to his cell and shortly afterward, he was released to return home to his family.

Every morning, for seventeen years, Dmitri sang his heart song. In the face of intense opposition and persecution, he offered praise to God. In the darkest and most hopeless of circumstances, he clung to the Lord Jesus and proclaimed his faith.

By all outward appearances, Dmitri's prison "ministry" was fruitless. He was one man, surrounded by evil, clinging to a God who seemed to have forgotten him. But because Dmitri lived to tell his story, we know better. Through Dmitri's testimony, we see an inside glimpse of the beauty of faith in the face of persecution.

"Everyone who wants to live a godly life in Christ Jesus will be persecuted," Paul reminded Timothy in 2 Timothy 3:12. "You, however, know all about my . . . persecutions, sufferings—what kinds of things happened to me in Antioch, Iconium and Lystra, the persecutions I endured. Yet the Lord rescued me from all of them" (vv. 10–11, 13). Even when all others deserted him, Paul testified, "the Lord stood at my side and gave me strength" (4:17).

I pray we'll never suffer for our faith as Paul did and Dmitri has, but we might. Will we have the courage to resolutely stand for Christ while the world rejects Him? Will we have joy that surpasses our trials and makes an impression on those around us? If we're steeped in God's Word like these men were, we will. Only biblical truth can give us hope to stand strong during persecution and difficulty.

God's Word gives us sure and certain hope that the same Spirit who empowered Dmitri, Paul, and countless believers down through the ages will also strengthen us.

And if the fires of persecution never touch our clothes? We can glorify God as we suffer in other ways, whether we have health crises, job losses, wayward children, or broken marriages, or whether we experience financial ruin, infertility, loneliness, or depression. Every day, we can lift our heart songs to God. The joy that transcends circumstances will enable us to sing because we rest in the shadow of His wings. Even if we don't sing aloud, we can testify through our actions and words that our faith is strong.

God will enable us to remain faithful in prayer and refuse to lose hope. He'll empower us to serve Him despite our heartache and proclaim His goodness to anyone who will listen. Our lives of faith will become our songs of praise for the watching world to hear.

Because of God's Word and the Holy Spirit who lives within us, we can hope to stand—joy filled and strong—during persecution and trials.

Take Heart

We may not feel strong or courageous now, but if we've steeped our minds in God's truth, we will stand strong when the fires of persecution and trials blaze.

From the Heart

Father, when I hear stories of Christians standing firm in the face of opposition and persecution, I marvel at their faith. I wonder, if I were in their places, if I'd have any hope of behaving so courageously. You suffered so much for me. If I'm ever called to suffer for your name, I want to make you proud. Help me prepare now by filling my mind with your Word so I'll have truth to strengthen me, not only to face persecution, but to be a faithful witness every day of my life. In the strong name of Jesus I ask, amen.

57

Sowing Tears, Reaping Joy

Those who sow with tears will reap with songs of joy. Those who go out weeping, carrying seed to sow, will return with songs of joy, carrying sheaves with them.

PSALM 126:5-6

On November 15, 2010, I read Psalm 126 and wept. "Those who sow with tears will reap with songs of joy. Those who go out weeping, carrying seed to sow, will return with songs of joy, carrying sheaves with them" (vv. 5–6).

I wept because this joyous promise seemed impossible. Heavy on my heart was my almost-adult child, who was so far from God I feared she'd never find her way back. I knew she couldn't wait to go off to college and live unencumbered by her parents' rules and standards.

The promise of Psalm 126 might be true in other situations, but my hopeless and heartbroken soul couldn't imagine that I'd ever be shouting for joy.

In the tears of that morning—not the first and not the last—God's Spirit drew close. The familiar weight of my Bible resting in my lap held a credibility I couldn't deny. So many promises. So much truth. So much history and evidence of God's work in the world. So many stories of transformation and redemption.

Almost in spite of myself, I felt a flicker of hope. Faith like a tiny flame pushed back the darkness of my grief and warmed my soul. "Faith is the assurance of things hoped for," the Spirit whispered, "the conviction of things not seen" (Hebrews 11:1 ESV).

Words from Romans 4 fanned the feeble flicker. "Against all hope, Abraham in hope believed" (v. 18). The Spirit added tinder from the book of Hebrews to the fire He'd sparked. "He who promised is faithful" (Hebrews 10:23). As the faith flame caught and grew, I picked up a pen and wrote in the margin, *Lord, I claim this promise for my child.*

Years before I'd begun the spiritual discipline of reading through the Bible every year. This practice became my daily source of strength. Whenever I'd grow weary or afraid, God would provide truth or comfort in His Word. And every November 15 following that prayer time, I'd read Psalm 126's hope-filled words and affirm the declaration I'd penned in the margin. *Lord, I claim this promise for my child.*

In the years that followed, I met once a month with other moms to share hope from the Scriptures and pray for our adult children. We reminded ourselves of God's heart for the lost and His power to save. I prayed with my church family, too. Many had family members and friends who weren't walking with the Lord. We'd often quote Psalm 126 to encourage ourselves.

I've come to realize this promise isn't only for brokenhearted mamas with wayward children. It encompasses anyone with a heart for God who eagerly desires a spiritual harvest.

Pastors cling to this promise as they battle the attacks of culture, politics, and evil. Missionaries who serve the kingdom far from home take comfort from its words. Marketplace Christians shining their faith lights into the dark places of our world find courage in the hope it offers. *Lord use our tears to water the faith seeds we're planting,* they pray. *Grow them into a bountiful harvest.*

Years had passed since I wrote my declaration of faith in my Bible. Some seasons were heartbreaking, and others were sprinkled with happiness and glimmers of hope. On the night of November 18, 2018, I settled into my cozy recliner and opened my One Year Bible. I'd fallen a few days behind in my Bible reading, but in God's perfect timing, my bookmark rested on November 15's reading—Psalm 126. I hadn't thought about the psalm in months, but there it was, with my prayer beside it.

As they had in times past, my tears flowed. But this time, they were tears of joy.

In the serendipitous timing only God could orchestrate, I read the words again, "Those who sow with tears will reap with songs of joy. Those who go out weeping, carrying seed to sow, will return with songs of joy, carrying sheaves with them" (Psalm 126:5–6).

My heart swelled with humble gratitude as I picked up my pen and wrote, *November 18, 2018 ~ I saw the fulfillment of this promise today. My daughter and her husband were baptized. Great is thy faithfulness.*

I read the rest of the psalm through swimmy eyes, "When the LORD restored the fortunes of Zion, we were like those who dreamed. Our mouths were filled with laughter, our tongues with songs of joy. Then it was said among the nations, 'The LORD has done great things for them.' The LORD has done great things for us, and we are filled with joy" (vv. 1–3).

Whether you're praying for a prodigal or ministering to the lost (or the saved) in some other way, you can live in hope that God will use the seeds you sow to accomplish His perfect will. You can trust that the Lord of the harvest will use your tears to water His kingdom fields and bring forth a bountiful crop.

Take Heart

God promises to replace our tears of sorrowful sowing with times of joyful reaping.

From the Heart

Precious and faithful Father, I don't know how many tears I've shed in this faith life, but you do. Scripture tells me you collect them in your bottle. Thank you for the promise of Psalm 126 that one day my tears will turn to joy. Help me persevere in faith. Strengthen me when I lose hope. When I'm tempted to despair, speak truth to my fainting heart. In your infinite wisdom, draw those I love to yourself. Advance your kingdom through me and other faithful witnesses. In the mighty name of Jesus I ask, amen.

Jesus Will Return

At that time they will see the
Son of Man coming in a cloud with
power and great glory.

LUKE 21:27

Elizabeth and Mike had been divorced for quite some time. In the days following their breakup, Mike had faithfully kept his commitment to the visitation schedule the court had set up for their son, John. Every other weekend, for two weeks in the summer, and on alternating holidays, Mike showed up at Elizabeth's front door to collect his son. He worked hard to maintain their relationship and shared the responsibilities of raising their six-year-old.

As time passed, however, Mike's visits became more sporadic. He'd call at the last minute and say something had come up or that he'd been called in to work. Sometimes he didn't have an excuse. He'd just say he wasn't coming to pick up John that weekend.

One day Elizabeth's cell phone rang. Seeing Mike's name on the caller ID, she handed the phone to John.

"Hey, Buddy, I've got tickets to the Mets game." Mike's voice boomed through the speaker. "I'll pick you up around ten. We can grab pizza afterward at Howie's."

They talked for a few minutes about batting averages and whether to have pepperoni or sausage on their pizza, then Mike clicked off. John tossed the phone to Elizabeth and pumped the air. His eyes shone brighter than they had in a long time.

When Elizabeth went to John's room the next morning to awaken him, she found him dressed in his New York Mets shirt and ball cap. His glove and ball sat beside him on the bed. Head in his hands and elbows on the windowsill, he watched through the window for his dad to arrive.

"Oh, honey," she said, wrapping her arm around his thin shoulders and giving him a squeeze, "your daddy's not coming for a couple of hours."

"I know, Mom," he said. "I just want to be ready."

You already know the ending to this sad story. John's dad never showed up. He called an hour before bedtime to say he'd been helping a friend work on his car and lost track of time. They'd do it another time.

John snatched the hat from his head, threw it into the corner, and flung himself, facedown, on his bed. Instead of lying awake in excitement, he cried himself to sleep.

Sadly, this scenario plays itself out in homes across the country every day. And not just homes that have been broken by divorce. If we swapped stories, we could all share times when an unkept promise weakened our trust, stole our hope, and broke our hearts.

I'm so grateful God keeps His promises. And that He never stands us up. Luke 21 records one of the most hope-filled promises in the Bible—the promise of Christ's return.

Jesus himself described His second coming this way: "There will be signs in the sun, moon and stars. On the earth, nations will be in anguish and perplexity at the roaring and tossing of the sea. People will faint from terror, apprehensive of what is coming on the world, for the heavenly bodies will be shaken. At that time they will see the Son of Man coming in a cloud with power and great glory. When these things begin to take place, stand up and lift up your heads, because your redemption is drawing near" (vv. 25–28).

No longer the suffering servant, Christ will come as a conquering King and a righteous ruler. Governments will crumble before Him. Armies will flee. Every knee will bow and every tongue will confess that Jesus Christ is Lord.

When the world seems hell-bent on its own destruction, I find great hope in knowing that God, not sinful mankind, orchestrates the events of our times. Because He's all-powerful, we can trust Him to shepherd the panorama of world affairs until they culminate in His triumphant and victorious return. And because He cannot lie, we can rest in confident expectation that He will do everything He has promised.

He'll resurrect our mortal bodies, reward our service, and usher us into His heavenly kingdom. He'll reveal to us the place He's been preparing for us, and there we will live with the Lord forever.

As John watched for his father, we, too, should watch for our heavenly Father. We can remain alert to signs of the times and biblical prophecy and "always be prepared to give an answer to everyone who asks you to give the reason for the hope that you have" (1 Peter 3:15).

Because we know He's coming, we can continue to serve Him, hope-filled and strong, as we rest in the promise of His return.

Take Heart

Jesus won't disappoint us. He will come again.

From the Heart

Lord, sometimes this world is scary. It's easy to forget you're in control. But knowing that you will one day return gives me hope for the future. Thank you for being a Father who keeps His promises to His children. Even so, come quickly, Lord Jesus!

59

Goodbyes Aren't Forever

And so we will be with the Lord forever.

1 THESSALONIANS 4:17

I hugged my daughter one last time—too tightly and for too long—before she settled behind the wheel of her trusty Toyota.

"Drive safely. Stop if you need to. Text me when you get home." I'd said these words a dozen times, but they never got easier. That day I squeezed them past a lump in my throat the size of Montana.

"Thanks for everything, Mom," my daughter said. "Don't worry. I'll be home soon."

And with a whoosh, she was gone. I plastered on a wobbly grin and waved as she drove away. If she looked back, I wanted her to see me smiling.

The taillights vanished around a bend, and my brave face crumbled. A sob hiccupped its way out of my chest. I lowered my arm as the tears I'd been holding in all morning fell in twin streams down my cheeks.

"I hate waving at taillights," I whispered. "I hate it. I hate it. I hate it."

My logical mind knows it's healthy and good for adult children to leave home and take their place in the world, but I'd be lying if I told you I enjoyed it. Being separated from someone I love always hurts.

I've experienced a similar grief as conflict divided me from family and friends. I've shed a sea of tears when military deployments transported my kids half a world away. And I've mourned deeply when disease and death snatched away those dear to me.

But one day—one glorious day—those of us who belong to Christ will never be separated again. From the babe in the womb who never drew a breath to the faithful senior who served God for a lifetime, we'll join the throng of the redeemed to live forever in God's presence. Herein we find hope.

"For the Lord himself will come down from heaven, with a loud command, with the voice of the archangel and with the trumpet call of God, and the dead in Christ will rise first. After that, we who are still alive and are left will be caught up together with them in the clouds to meet the Lord in the air. *And so we will be with the Lord forever*" (1 Thessalonians 4:16–17, emphasis added).

No more painful goodbyes. No more wishing for what might have been. No more *If only we'd had more time.*

Forever will begin. Eternity will eclipse the earthly and time will cease. The grandest, most glorious family reunion will commence and never stop.

Brothers and sisters in Christ will gather around the Father's table and link arms in a group hug that will span the ages. Unlike in the family portrait where someone's always frowning, every face will be radiant as we reflect our Father's glory.

Imagine this the next time you say goodbye to someone you love—for a short time or a long one. Find hope and strength in God's promise.

Wave at the taillights. Shed the tears. But cling to the solid hope that if your loved one knows Jesus, your goodbye is only temporary.

And don't worry. They'll be home soon.

One day, as Jesus promised, "we will be with the Lord forever" (1 Thessalonians 4:17).

Take Heart

Even "permanent" goodbyes are temporary when Christ lives in our hearts.

From the Heart

Father, I hate goodbyes. I really, really hate them. Help me remember that one day, perhaps sooner than I imagine, this sad, broken world will end, and we'll join you in heaven forever. Draw my loved ones to yourself so we can gather around your table—together—forever. Help me live in hope of an eternal existence surrounded by my loved ones and free from goodbyes.

60

Incomparable Glory Awaits Us

> I consider that our present sufferings
> are not worth comparing with
> the glory that will be revealed in us.

ROMANS 8:18

Do you ever look down the long list of prayer needs at church and feel hopeless? Cancer, Alzheimer's, broken marriages, troubled teenagers, suicide, child abuse, unemployment, human trafficking, and a thousand other manifestations of sin in our world can quickly rob us of hope and peace.

And what if the long list of trials belongs to you? If the cancer's in your body? The rebellious child sleeps under your roof? The crumbling marriage has your *I do* attached to it?

What do you do when grief nearly capsizes you, but you manage to climb aboard a life raft, only to discover sharks encircling you? How do you cling to hope when danger closes in?

You talk to someone who can offer truly dependable answers.

When I needed effective ways to soothe a colicky baby, I sought advice from a mother of five. When my daughter's teeth needed straightening, I took her to an orthodontist. When my car engine spewed steam, I called a mechanic.

When our spirits grow weary and we fear we can't go on, God's Word provides a staggering list of believers who walked through the fire of life's trials with their hope intact. The apostle Paul is one of them.

Listen to the Cliff Notes version of his life after coming to Christ. Read slowly and think about each experience. Imagine what even one of Paul's trials would feel like:

> I have worked much harder, been in prison more frequently, been flogged more severely, and been exposed to death again and again. Five times I received from the Jews the forty lashes minus one. Three times I was beaten with rods, once I was pelted with stones, three times I was shipwrecked, I spent a night and a day in the open sea, I have been constantly on the move. I have been in danger from rivers, in danger from bandits, in danger from my fellow Jews, in danger from Gentiles; in danger in the city, in danger in the country, in danger at sea; and in danger from false believers. I have labored and toiled and have often gone without sleep; I have known hunger and thirst and have often gone without food; I have been cold and naked. Besides everything else, I face daily the pressure of my concern for all the churches. (2 Corinthians 11:23–28)

How did Paul press on in hope until he could say with certainty, "I have fought the good fight, I have finished the race, I have kept the faith" (2 Timothy 4:7)?

Paul knew a secret that wasn't really a secret. He shared it in Romans 8:18: "I consider that our present sufferings are not worth comparing with the glory that will be revealed in us."

The trials? The heartache? The sickness and pain? The struggle to live godly in an ungodly world? The battles with the world, the flesh, and the devil? They're a speck of dirt in an ant's eye. A millisecond of eternity. A whisp of dandelion fluff compared to what eternity holds for us.

This truth gave Paul hope. It grants us hope, too.

"For the creation waits in eager expectation for the children of God to be revealed. For the creation was subjected to frustration, not by its own choice, but by the will of the one who subjected it, *in hope* that the creation itself will be liberated from its bondage to decay and brought into the freedom and glory of the children of God" (Romans 8:19–21, emphasis added).

One day we'll be liberated from sin, sorrow, sickness, and death. From the constant battle between the flesh and the spirit. We'll be released to live as God intended us to live—able to walk and talk with God in His presence again, free from sin forever. We'll become everything He created us to be.

This hope of glory seems unimaginable, yet it is as certain as God himself, because He promised it. Paul saw this future glory with his spiritual eyes. God allows us to glimpse it as well. Tucked into the pages of Scripture are thousands of glimmers of future hope and glory like this sneak peek just waiting for us to discover them.

Read them. Believe them. Take hope in them because incomparable glory awaits us.

Take Heart

The promise of an endless future filled with unimaginable glory provides the hope we need to navigate our darkest days.

From the Heart

Some days, Lord, the only thing that keeps me from giving up is knowing that a better future awaits me. I long for a time when the suffering and heartache of this life end and my forever future begins. Until then, Lord, keep me anchored in the hope I find in the glories you showed Paul. Thank you for allowing me to glimpse these glories through his eyes and through your Word. In the strong name of Jesus I ask, amen.

How to Have a
Relationship with Christ

The Bible tells us how:

We must understand that we have sinned, and that our sin grieves and separates us from our loving Father God.

For all have sinned and fall short of the glory of God (Romans 3:23).

Because we are sinners, we are separated from God and deserve to die and spend eternity in hell.

For the wages of sin is death (Romans 6:23).

We can't do anything to earn our place in heaven.

For it is by grace you have been saved, through faith—and this is not from yourselves, it is the gift of God—not by works, so that no one can boast (Ephesians 2:8–9).

God loved us so much that He sacrificed his sinless, perfect Son, Jesus, to pay for our sin.

For God so loved the world that he gave his one and only Son, that whoever believes in him shall not perish but have eternal life (John 3:16).

God made him who had no sin to be sin for us, so that in him we might become the righteousness of God (2 Corinthians 5:21).

We must be willing to repent of (turn away from) our sin and accept by faith what Jesus did for us on the cross. When we do this, God promises us a relationship with Him and a forever home in heaven. *But the gift of God is eternal life in Christ Jesus our Lord* (Romans 6:23).

If you want to have a relationship with God, tell Him.

Here's a sample prayer:

"God, I know I'm a sinner who doesn't deserve a place in your heaven. Today I repent of my sin. I surrender my life to you. I accept what Jesus did for me when He died on the cross. Come into my heart, God, and make me a new person."

If you prayed this prayer, or said the same thing in your own words, and really meant it, God has something to say to you:

> If you declare with your mouth, "Jesus is Lord," and believe in your heart that God raised him from the dead, you will be saved. (Romans 10:9)

If you surrendered your life to Christ, I want to rejoice with you and help you on your way. Please drop me an email at LoriAHatcher @gmail.com. For more encouragement, visit my blog, *Refresh*, at www .LoriHatcher.com.

Notes

Introduction

1. J. I. Packer and Carolyn Nystrom, *Never beyond Hope: How God Touches and Uses Imperfect People* (Downers Grove, IL: InterVarsity Press, 2000), 15.
2. C. H. Spurgeon, "Unanswered Prayer (no. 3344)," Christian Classics Ethereal Library, accessed July 14, 2021, https://ccel .org/ccel/spurgeon/sermons59/sermons59.x.html.

Part 1: God's Nature (Who God Is)

1. "Death Row to Abundant Life: Jimmy MacPhee," On the Rock Ministries, accessed October 13, 2020, https://ontherockjimmy .org/.
2. Max Anders, *Holman New Testament Commentary: Galatians, Ephesians, Philippians and Colossians* (Nashville: Holman Reference, 1984), 262.
3. Rebecca Shinners, "What It's Like to Experience One of America's Oldest Fourth of July Celebrations," *Country Living*, July 6, 2015, https://www.countryliving.com/life/travel/a35874 /americas-oldest-4th-of-july-celebration/.
4. C. H. Spurgeon, "Justification by Faith (no. 3392)," Christian Classics Ethereal Library, accessed November 9, 2021, https: //ccel.org/ccel/spurgeon/sermons60/sermons60.vi.html.

5. Heather Mercer, "Captured by the Taliban," The Hope Center, January 17, 2017, YouTube video, https://www.youtube.com /watch?v=GJdEZUENtj0.

6. Mercer, "Captured by the Taliban."

7. John MacArthur, *The MacArthur Daily Bible* (Nashville: Thomas Nelson, 2003), 846.

8. Thomas Watson, *All Things for Good: A Puritan Guide* (Las Vegas: Olahauski Bodes, 2021), 19.

9. Michael Hingson, "A Blind Man, His Guide Dog and Lessons Learned on 9/11," Fox News, May 7, 2015, https://www .foxnews.com/opinion/a-blind-man-his-guide-dog-and-lessons -learned-on-9-11; the author also attended an event at which Hingson presented his story.

10. Hingson, "Blind Man"; event with Hingson.

Part 2: God's Work (What God Does)

1. Joanna Walters, "'The Happening': 10 Years after the Amish Shooting," *The Guardian*, October 2, 2016, https://www .theguardian.com/us-news/2016/oct/02/amish-shooting-10 -year-anniversary-pennsylvania-the-happening.

2. Terri Roberts, "Forgiven: The Amish School Shooting, a Mother's Love, and a Story of Remarkable Grace," Bethany House, September 21, 2015, YouTube video, https://www .youtube.com/watch?v=oEiRZZtVcjY&t=1s.

3. Roberts, "Forgiven."

4. Roberts, "Forgiven."

5. Marie Monville, "Amish School Shooter's Widow Finds Peace in God," The 700 Club, October 17, 2013, YouTube video, https://www.youtube.com/watch?v=IDmi-o7X-vM.

6. Mike Valerio, "Tomb of the Unknown Soldier Sentinels Continue Their Duty through Coronavirus Pandemic," WUSA9, March 24, 2020, https://www.wusa9.com/article /news/health/coronavirus/tomb-of-the-unknown-soldier -coronavirus/65-92ccf662-ac24-4a32-a8a5-14f8b86d466f.

Part 3: God's Word (What God Says)

1. "Billy Graham's Life and Ministry by the Numbers," Lifeway Research, February 21, 2018, https://research.lifeway .com/2018/02/21/billy-grahams-life-ministry-by-the-numbers/.

2. Linda Van Deusen, in discussion with the author, June 2010; all subsequent quotations in this devotion were recorded during this interview.

3. E.V. Hill, "How to Make the Enemy Run," Memorize Truth, November 13, 2007, YouTube video, https://www.youtube.com /watch?v=O6vL6DwrPaQ.

4. "Who Were the Sons of Korah in the Old Testament?," GotQuestions.org, accessed November 6, 2021, https://www .gotquestions.org/sons-of-Korah.html.

5. Nik Ripken with Gregg Lewis, *The Insanity of God: A True Story of Faith Resurrected* (Nashville: B&H Publishing Group, 2013), 156.

6. Ripken, *The Insanity of God*, 156.

7. Ripken, 156.

About the Author

Lori Hatcher is an author, blogger, pastor's wife, career health-care worker, and women's ministry speaker. She's partnering with Our Daily Bread Publishing to create a devotional series, which includes *Refresh Your Faith: Uncommon Devotions from Every Book of the Bible*, *Refresh Your Prayers: Uncommon Devotions to Restore Power and Praise*, and now *Refresh Your Hope: 60 Devotions for Trusting God with All Your Heart*.

Lori's articles and devotions have appeared in numerous print and online publications including *Our Daily Bread*, *The Upper Room*, *Guideposts*, *Revive Our Hearts*, and Crosswalk.com. She's contributed to compilations such as *God Loves Her*, *All God's Creatures*, *Guideposts One-Minute Daily Devotional*, *Evenings with Jesus*, and *God Hears Her*, *A Joyful Christmas*.

A contest-winning Toastmasters International speaker (ACG, ALB), Lori uses high-impact stories to impart transformational truth. She often draws from her childhood in small-town Rhode Island, her work as a dental hygienist, and the spiritual insights she gains from her grandchildren to create touching stories that reveal God's love and character.

Since Lori came to faith at age eighteen, her goal has been to "always be prepared to give an answer to everyone who asks you to give the reason for the hope that you have" (1 Peter 3:15). This goal became the inspiration for *Refresh Your Hope*. It is her prayer that on its pages you'll find unshakable reasons not to lose heart, no matter what storms come your way.

If *Refresh Your Hope* blessed you, Lori would be most grateful if you'd leave a review on Amazon.com or your favorite book retailer. Thoughtful reviews help readers find great books.

If you'd like to learn more about Lori and her well-loved 5-minute devotions, visit LoriHatcher.com.

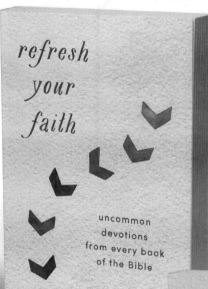

refresh
your
faith

uncommon
devotions
from every book
of the Bible

Lori Hatcher

Also from
Lori Hatcher

refresh
your
prayers

uncommon
devotions
to restore
power and praise

Lori Hatcher

Spread the Word
by Doing One Thing.

- Give a copy of this book as a gift.

- Share the QR code link via your social media.

- Write a review of this book on your blog, favorite bookseller's website, or at ODB.org/store.

- Recommend this book to your church, small group, or book club.

Connect with us. [f] [○] [𝕐]

Our Daily Bread Publishing
PO Box 3566, Grand Rapids, MI 49501, USA
Email: books@odb.org